VIRGIL AENEID X

EDITED WITH INTRODUCTION,
NOTES AND VOCABULARY
BY R.H. JORDAN
SENIOR CLASSICS MASTER, METHODIST COLLEGE, BELFAST

PUBLISHED BY BRISTOL CLASSICAL PRESS
GENERAL EDITOR: JOHN H. BETTS

To James Harrison
former colleague, mentor and friend

This impression 2005
First published in 1990 by
Bristol Classical Press
an imprint of
Gerald Duckworth & Co. Ltd.
90-93 Cowcross Street, London EC1M 6BF
Tel: 020 7490 7300
Fax: 020 7490 0080
inquiries@duckworth-publishers.co.uk
www.ducknet.co.uk

A catalogue record for this book is available
from the British Library

ISBN 1-85399-045-0

Printed and bound in Great Britain by
Antony Rowe Ltd, Eastbourne

Contents

Foreword

Book X of the Aeneid is possibly the least read of the whole poem; this is a pity as it contains much beautiful and forceful poetry and presents incidents which are important to the story. This edition has been designed to be of use to both GCSE and A level students.

The Introduction deals briefly with Virgil's life and various topics related to the poem as a whole; a select bibliography is provided. There is a full Vocabulary, and the Notes are designed to give help in translating the Latin and in gaining an appreciation of the poetry.

The two Appendices give help with Virgil's metre and the scansion of the lines, but it is hoped that the Latin will be read aloud. To ignore the sound of the poetry is to lose much of its force and even some of its meaning.

The text used in the preparation of this edition is substantially that to be found in the Oxford Classical Text of F.A. Hirtzel (1900). Help was also found in the commentary of R.D. Williams Books VII-XII (London 1973).

Thanks are due to Unwin Hyman for permission to use copyright material from their *Ovid on Himself* by J.A. Harrison. G.C. Cooper's *An Introduction to the Latin Hexameter* (Macmillan) was also useful in the scansion appendices. I owe a special debt firstly to James Harrison, to whom this volume is dedicated, for the considerable assistance he gave me on its first draft, and secondly to my colleague John McNee who read much of this edition and made many helpful suggestions.

Finally I must thank also the Bristol Classical Press whose reader and General Editor gave me valuable help and encouragement.

R.H.J.
Belfast

Introduction

Publius Vergilius Maro – better known by the anglicised form of his gentile name as Virgil – was born near Mantua in northern Italy on October 15th 70 BC. His father is said to have been a small farmer but he must have been not without means since his son, after primary education in Cremona and Mediolanum (Milan), studied Greek at Neapolis (Naples) and philosophy and rhetoric at Rome. It seems he returned home on the completion of his education and may have written such minor works as *Ciris*, *Copa* and others.

After the defeat of Brutus and Cassius at Philippi in 42 BC, Virgil's father was evicted from his farm. The youthful poet, however, won the favour of Asinius Pollio, governor of Cisalpine Gaul, to whom he dedicated his first major work, the ten *Eclogues*, pastoral poems imitating those of the Greek poet Theocritus. Pollio introduced Virgil to Octavian, the future emperor Augustus, as a result of which the family farm was possibly restored.

Virgil now lived mostly at Naples. He was now a friend of the emperor and a member of the exclusive set which gathered round the great literary patron Maecenas. Virgil followed the *Eclogues* with four books of *Georgics* (dealing with farming, livestock, trees and bee-keeping). These were not merely lists of advice for farmers but an artistic masterpiece showing Virgil's love of the countryside and his mastery of the hexameter metre. The 2184 lines took him seven years to write, so carefully was each line polished and revised.

Virgil's great epic, the *Aeneid*, discussed in the next section of this book, was commissioned by Augustus himself and occupied the last eleven years of Virgil's life. He died at Brundisium (Brindisi) on his way home from a visit to Greece in 19 BC and was buried at Naples. The *Aeneid* had not received its finishing touches and the poet wished it to be destroyed. Augustus forbade this and ordered the poem to be published.

We know little of Virgil's personal life. Technically he was born a Gaul, for the people of Cisalpine Gaul only later received Roman citizenship. In the Middle Ages he was considered to be a sort of wizard, for did not the fourth *Eclogue* foretell the birth of Christ? Men seeking guidance about the future sought his advice by opening his works at random. Virgil himself was a shy, introverted person who seldom visited Rome and once ran into a nearby house to avoid a crowd who had recognised him. And yet the poet Horace, whose character was in every way the opposite of Virgil's, counted him as a very dear friend – 'half of my life' he calls him. We can imagine him, in the quietness of his Neapolitan home working on his great epic year after year, burnishing his brilliant hexameters and, in the end, dying not totally satisfied with his efforts.

In the last stanza of his *Ode to Virgil* Tennyson pays him a fitting tribute,

> 'I salute thee, Mantovano,
> I that loved thee since my day began,
> Wielder of the stateliest measure
> Ever moulded by the lips of man.'

THE AENEID

The *Aeneid* is a great national epic in twelve books telling how Aeneas, a Trojan prince, and other survivors from the destruction of Troy by the Greeks in the Trojan War left their homeland and sailed westwards to found a new city that would be more famous than Troy itself. In this Virgil was greatly influenced by the Homeric poems (see 'Virgil and his Predecessors' below). The first six books are largely taken up by the wanderings of the Trojans and can be termed Virgil's *Odyssey*. They need not concern us greatly here as it is the war in Italy occupying the second half of the poem (Virgil's *Iliad*) which is our main interest.

Book VII opens with the poet invoking the Muse afresh to tell of wars. At first everything seems favourable. King Latinus, who has been told in an oracle that his daughter Lavinia should marry a foreigner, promises her to Aeneas. The goddess Juno, however, still hostile to the Trojans, incites Amata, King Latinus' wife, and Turnus, leader of the powerful Rutulian tribe, to oppose the marriage. Turnus himself had been betrothed to Lavinia and so had some justification for his opposition.

At the beginning of the eighth book Aeneas is beset with problems. The river Tiber, however, appears to him in a vision and tells him to go upstream and ask for help from Evander, whose settlement is on the future site of Rome. Evander willingly offers help. He sends his son Pallas to fight on the Trojan side and urges Aeneas to visit Tarchon, the Etruscan king, and raise more allies.

Book IX relates the events that take place around the Trojan camp during Aeneas' absence. There the Trojans, led by Ascanius, Aeneas' son, are besieged in their camp by the Latins, led by Turnus. The situation becomes desperate and the camp holds out with great difficulty. This prompts two young Trojans, Nisus and Euryalus, to set out through the enemy lines in an effort to reach Aeneas. Unfortunately, betrayed by the gleam of a helmet they are surrounded and die fighting. The ninth book ends with a furious onslaught on the Trojan camp by the Rutulians led by Turnus.

BOOK TEN

Wight Duff in his *Literary History of Rome* says, 'we could spare much of Book X', but this is too harsh a judgement. It is true that the long description of killings becomes a little tedious, since they do not have the lively inventiveness of similar passages in the *Iliad*, but there is plenty of fine poetry to admire and some of the events in this book are crucial for the poem as a whole.

As the previous book closed, success for the Trojan cause

seemed to be in doubt. Turnus and his forces were in the ascendant, so unless Aeneas and his allies can intervene with decisive force all looks lost. The opening lines of Book X, however, take the reader away to the spacious world of the gods. This acts as a contrast to the confined conditions of the Trojan camp and provides a majestic prelude to the first of this book's three sections – the return of Aeneas.

The scene on Olympus is not so long that it breaks the momentum of the story but long enough for Venus and Juno to register their bitter protests and for Jupiter to issue an important edict. Some of what he says is a little obscure, but three things are clear: (i) Jupiter will be impartial to all – a rebuff for the two warring goddesses, (ii) each person by his own actions will bring his own suffering or good fortune, and (iii) the Fates will bring matters to their conclusion. The second point prepares us for what will happen to the leading characters in the story, in particular Pallas, Lausus, Mezentius and Turnus. After Jupiter's edict we return to earth and the helpless Trojans penned inside their fort. In less than thirty lines Virgil reminds us of the current state of the conflict and the plight of the defenders, cataloguing some of them by name in traditional epic style. Everything in the book so far increases the reader's anticipation of Aeneas' arrival.

At last Aeneas appears, sailing at the head of the reinforcements. The excitement of this episode is carefully built up in a number of ways. Firstly the poet summarises Aeneas' travels since he left Evander at the end of Book VIII. Then, after an invocation of the Muses, he catalogues in a style reminiscent of Homer (cf. *Iliad* Book II) the contingents that are accompanying Aeneas. Finally the poet describes the divine escort of sea nymphs who were once part of the Trojan fleet.

Now the scene is set up for the climax of this section of the book. Aeneas raises his divine shield to signal his arrival and the beleaguered Trojans shout with relief. In contrast Turnus and the Latins gaze out to sea in bewilderment at the mass of ships heading for the shore. Virgil marks the high point in the narrative by a concentration of ominous similes and his description of Aeneas is couched in mystical and semi-religious imagery. This section of the book is rounded off by a landing from the ships in the teeth of vigorous resistance. Aeneas confirms the ominous similes by killing a series of opponents each of whom are treated to a brief stylized description.

The second section deals with the fighting on the shore and concentrates on Pallas, the son of Aeneas' new ally Evander. As the section opens, the Arcadians are in disarray and about to flee but Pallas raises their fighting spirit by dashing into the thick of the battle and killing a succession of opponents. As the battle rages, Turnus makes his entry and demands to face Pallas alone. Virgil begins to prepare us for the outcome with a simile of Turnus as a lion. Pallas invokes the aid of Hercules but Hercules knows that he can do nothing. Jupiter consoles Hercules saying that he too lost a son, Sarpedon, at Troy and adds that Turnus too has reached the end of his life. In the duel Pallas manages to pierce Turnus' shield and graze him. As the narrative increases in dramatic intensity and detail, Turnus fatally wounds Pallas with his spear and in traditional fashion stands over him to glory in his moment of victory. With bitter words that match his character he tears Pallas' belt from his body as a trophy.

The killing of Pallas by Turnus is a turning point in the poem motivating the rest of the action. By ripping the belt from Pallas to wear himself, Turnus seals his own future death at the hands of Aeneas, for this tips the scales against him in Book XII when Aeneas has him at his mercy. Also Pallas' death produces in Aeneas an insane fury, expressed in a rampage of killing which brings the second section of the book to a close. Here Virgil portrays a different view of Aeneas' character, one totally at variance with the 'pietas' he has so often demonstrated up to now. Several of the enemy beg him for mercy but he despatches them with a vindictive savagery not seen before. As if to leave us in no doubt, the poet has Aeneas rounding up eight young men to sacrifice later at Pallas' burial.

In the third and final section of Book X, we perhaps expect the final confrontation between Aeneas and Turnus. Both men,

Aeneas in particular, are actively looking for each other but Virgil deftly postpones the confrontation substituting Lausus and Mezentius his father as opponents for Aeneas. This section opens with a very short prelude set on Olympus. Jupiter teases a dejected Juno but finally allows her to prolong Turnus' life for a short time by stealing him away from the battlefield. To do this Juno forms a misty wraith in the form of Aeneas which lures Turnus onto a ship. Juno then sets the ship adrift and it floats out to sea carrying a confused and deluded Turnus out of reach of his foe. It is interesting to note that Juno had reproached Venus at the beginning of this book for using a mist to rescue Aeneas from the Greeks at Troy.

When the reader returns to the battlefield he finds that Mezentius, the exiled Etruscan tyrant, has taken Turnus' place at the head of the Latin forces. This warrior is described in fearsome terms with very powerful similes: a boar, a ravenous lion and Orion; he is someone left over from a less civilised time, a ruthless warrior and someone who disdains the gods. The fighting continues with Mezentius resolutely withstanding the fierce onslaught of his former subjects and killing a succession of opponents. In due course Mezentius meets Aeneas and is forced to retire, wounded by Aeneas' spear. At the dramatic moment when Aeneas is about to finish Mezentius off, Lausus loyally rushes to his rescue enabling his father to withdraw from battle to nurse his wound.

The ensuing encounter between the young Lausus and Aeneas and its sequel form the finale to the book and Virgil produces some of his finest poetry to match its dramatic and highly moving moments. After his encounter with Lausus, Aeneas is shocked out of his savage fury. The sight of the pale face of the dying youth causes him to reflect on his own family – his father towards whom he had shown such 'pietas' and his son for whom he has a love equally as strong as that of Mezentius for Lausus. With a touch of remorse Aeneas himself lifts the dead youth and hands him back to his comrades. The inevitable sequel to this brings Book X to a close. Mezentius, weak from his wound, is presented with his son's dead body and overcome by desperate remorse resolves to return to the battle. In what follows Virgil paints for the reader a slightly different picture of Mezentius, for the warrior who can kill so ruthlessly is as vulnerable as anyone else. Now that Lausus is dead the only living thing he can show affection to is his horse, which he addresses by name and talks to in exactly the way he would a human comrade. He mounts with difficulty and rides off to battle for the last time. The fight is a furious affair with Aeneas caught under a barrage of spears until finally Aeneas strikes Mezentius' horse in the head with a spear. The horse rears and falls on top of Mezentius. Now at Aeneas' mercy Mezentius, like the professional soldier he was, has no fear of dying and asks for no mercy; he simply requests to be buried alongside his son.

THE SEQUEL

Book XI acts as an extended prelude to the final outcome of the story. The body of Pallas is taken home to his father Evander for burial and a twelve-day truce is made for the burial of the dead. The Latins then hold a council of war at which various policies are proposed, with Turnus advocating a continuation of the war. As they debate, news comes that the Trojans are on the move and war breaks out again. The rest of the book is devoted to a cavalry battle with the Latin forces who are commanded by Camilla, a warrior princess. Camilla is killed and the opposing armies encamp for the night.

The long-awaited confrontation between Turnus and Aeneas comes in Book XII and occupies almost the whole book. Turnus sees that the morale of his forces is broken and there remains no alternative to facing Aeneas in single combat. Latinus and Amata attempt to dissuade him but he is adamant. The confrontation, however, does not take place quickly; there is a slow build up with an elaborate description of Turnus arming himself, and a setback occurs when the Rutulians break the truce resulting in a period of renewed fighting between both armies. At first Turnus wreaks a terrible slaughter but soon Aeneas rallies the Trojans and tracks

Turnus down. Eventually they meet, and in an episode reminiscent of Achilles' fight with Hector in the *Iliad*, Aeneas wounds
Turnus in the thigh. As he is about to relent and grant Turnus his
life, he notices the belt stripped from Pallas on Turnus; in a
moment of blind rage Aeneas kills Turnus. So the poem ends on
a jarring note which many scholars in both ancient and more
modern times have found rather disconcerting.

VIRGIL AND HIS PREDECESSORS

In various fields of literature the Romans looked to the works of
earlier Greek writers as their models. For epic poetry the Homeric poems were masterpieces of such quality that all succeeding
writers, both Greek and Roman, felt obliged to acknowledge this
by re-using incidents and ideas taken from the *Iliad* and the
Odyssey.

In the *Aeneid* we find strong echoes of the Homeric poems. In
structure the early part of the *Aeneid* mirrors that of the *Odyssey*,
with Aeneas recounting his adventures for Dido just as Odysseus
does for Alcinous. Secondly, an important element in the final
books of the *Aeneid* is the vengeful anger Aeneas has towards
Turnus for the death of his young friend and ally Pallas. This
undoubtedly is based on the consuming anger Achilles has for
Hector in the *Iliad* because of the death of his friend Patroclus.
Other parallels easily come to mind. Both heroes, Odysseus and
Aeneas, visit the Underworld, though the land of the dead is
viewed quite differently in the two poems. There are funeral
games described in great detail for Patroclus in the *Iliad* and for
Anchises in the *Aeneid*. Two heroes, Achilles and Aeneas, are
presented with new suits of armour thanks to their mothers. In
Book II of the *Iliad* there is a long catalogue of the various
contingents of Greeks who made up the besieging army at Troy.
At the end of the seventh book of the *Aeneid* there is a similar
catalogue, but this time of the Italian contingents that massed to
oppose the Trojans.

The world of the Homeric poems is peopled by heroes,

impetuous individuals whose sole aim in life is to gain glory which is done chiefly through exploits in war. The common people are shadowy participants, serving either as nameless victims in battle or subjects over whom the heroes exercise their rule. Social obligations hardly exist in Homeric society; concern for another person is only possible in the case of someone of equal status. In Virgil, however, we enter a different world. As a hero, Aeneas disregards his own feelings and wishes to a large extent and demonstrates a compassionate concern for his family and the people under his care. Furthermore, Aeneas is conscious of his obligations to the gods and the future of his race to a much greater degree than any Homeric hero and, for this, he is often described by the poet as 'pius'.

The poet or poets of the Homeric poems are constantly looking backwards to a lost age of martial glory and power; in contrast, Virgil's poetry looks forward on two levels. Firstly, Aeneas spends little time and effort lamenting the past glories of Troy but looks to the future. The main warfare section of the *Aeneid* – Virgil's *Iliad* – is set significantly at the site of Troy's successor, whereas the fighting in the *Iliad* marks the end of an era and has as its object the restoration of a hero's honour. On the second level Virgil, through his description of a heroic past, was pointing the way forward to a new Rome after the destruction of the recent civil war.

Links between the *Aeneid* and the Homeric poems abound and are certain, but it is much more difficult to gauge whether Virgil drew on ideas from other Greek authors. For example, does Dido in Book IV of the *Aeneid* owe anything to Medea in the *Argonautica* of Apollonius Rhodius? However there is little doubt that Virgil's account of the Trojan wanderings after they left their ruined city follows very closely the route described in a work by Dionysius of Halicarnassus. It is impossible to tell whether Virgil owed anything to the Roman writers before him. This is due to the scanty fragments that remain of the hexameter *Annales* of Ennius and of Naevius' *Bellum Poenicum* written in Saturnian metre.

THE AENEID AND ROME

Virgil was writing the *Aeneid* at a time when the Roman world had recently emerged from a period of civil war. Many people's lives had been shattered, the old republican system swept away and Augustus established by conquest as supreme ruler of the Roman empire. There was a widespread longing for peace and an end to lawlessness, a return to the traditional Roman values which had made Rome great, even if the political institutions associated with them had gone for ever. The poet Horace, Virgil's contemporary, lamented the deserted and derelict state of many shrines which symbolised for him the moral bankruptcy of contemporary Roman society (*Odes* III 6). In response to this feeling Augustus, when he came to power, introduced not only political measures but also some social and religious ones to restore the shattered fabric of society. In the *Aeneid* Virgil provided some of the inspiration to rally the Roman people to a rebuilding of Rome's greatness.

Although Aeneas is nominally the hero of the poem, in many ways the real focus of attention is the future city – eventually to be Rome itself. For Aeneas it is the future home towards which he is leading his band of followers; for the poet it is a common inheritance of which the Romans of his day should feel justly proud. It is no accident that Virgil's story begins chronologically with the Trojan War, for this gave the Romans a claim to be as ancient as the Greeks and this, through Aeneas, provided them with divine ancestors. At the same time, in tune with the mood of Virgil's own day, the *Aeneid* portrays Aeneas, the archetypal Roman, leading a remnant shattered by war forwards into the future under the guidance of the gods. Thus the *Aeneid* is a poetic version of Rome's earliest history and an inspiration for the renewing of her way of life under the Augustan reforms.

Among various references to Roman history, the most obvious is that concerning Dido and Carthage in Book IV. Carthage for the Romans was a city of fearful memory, a power which came very close to destroying Rome under the leadership of Hannibal. Virgil capitalised on this by projecting the foundation of Carthage back in time and making Dido an insidious threat to the future destiny of Rome. Another reference occurs in Book VI when Aeneas is visiting the Underworld to see his father, Anchises. In the timeless setting of the land of the dead Virgil is able to recall the heroes of the Roman people from the earliest period right up to Julius Caesar, Pompeius and Augustus himself. The poet describes how Aeneas was inspired by the sight of these Romans waiting to be born and no doubt Virgil hoped that his readers also would be inspired in the same way.

Thirdly, in Book VIII Aeneas is presented by his mother, Venus, with a new suit of armour forged and decorated by Vulcan. On the shield various scenes from Roman history are depicted, with pride of place being given to the battle of Actium and to Augustus. Also, in Book VIII Evander, Aeneas' host, conducts Aeneas around the future site of the city of Rome pointing out features like the Tarpeian Rock and the Capitol, all very familiar to the Romans of Virgil's own day.

All these allusions serve the purpose of making the story thoroughly Roman in flavour as well as language, and they bind a legend which was essentially one of prehistory to the stream of Roman history. This gives the poem a reality and power which the story of a wandering hero could never have possessed, and transforms Aeneas into a true Roman of whom those of Virgil's day could justly feel proud.

Select Bibliography

This bibliography is divided into two sections: A is regarded as suitable for readers preparing for GCSE examinations at 15 + ; B is for older students.

SECTION A

Williams, R.D. *Aeneas and the Roman Hero* (Macmillan, 1973; Inside the Ancient World series).

Camps, W.A. *An Introduction to Virgil's Aeneid* (Oxford University Press, 1969).

Griffin, Jasper *Virgil* (Oxford University Press, 1986; Past Masters).

SECTION B

Quinn, K. *Virgil's* Aeneid, *a Critical Description* (Routledge & Kegan Paul, 1968).

Otis, Brooks *Virgil, a Study in Civilized Poetry* (Oxford University Press, 1964).

Gransden, K.W. *Virgil's* Iliad (Cambridge University Press, 1984).

Commager, Steele (ed.) *Virgil, a Collection of Critical Essays*, 20th Century views (Prentice-Hall, 1966).

Dudley, D.R. (ed.) *Virgil, Studies in Latin Literature and its Influence* (Routledge & Kegan Paul, 1969).

Hunt, J.W. *Forms of Glory* (South Illinois University Press, 1973).

Williams, G. *Technique and Ideas in the Aeneid* (Yale, 1983).

Aeneid Book X

Jupiter orders the gods to cease from strife until Carthage makes war on Rome.

Panditur interea domus omnipotentis Olympi,
conciliumque vocat divum pater atque hominum rex
sideream in sedem, terras unde arduus omnes
castraque Dardanidum aspectat populosque Latinos.
5   consident tectis bipatentibus; incipit ipse:
'caelicolae magni, quianam sententia vobis
versa retro, tantumque animis certatis iniquis?
abnueram bello Italiam concurrere Teucris.
quae contra vetitum discordia? quis metus aut hos
10   aut hos arma sequi ferrumque lacessere suasit?
adveniet iustum pugnae, ne arcessite, tempus,
cum fera Karthago Romanis arcibus olim
exitium magnum atque Alpes immittet apertas:
tum certare odiis, tum res rapuisse licebit.
15   nunc sinite; et placitum laeti componite foedus.'

Venus laments the woes of the Trojans and asks that Ascanius at least may be saved.

    Iuppiter haec paucis; at non Venus aurea contra
pauca refert:
'o pater, o hominum rerumque aeterna potestas!

1

namque aliud quid sit, quod iam implorare queamus?
20 cernis ut insultent Rutuli, Turnusque feratur
per medios insignis equis tumidusque secundo
Marte ruat? non clausa tegunt iam moenia Teucros.
quin intra portas atque ipsis proelia miscent
aggeribus murorum et inundant sanguine fossae.
25 Aeneas ignarus abest. nunquamne levari
obsidione sines? muris iterum imminet hostis
nascentis Troiae nec non exercitus alter;
atque iterum in Teucros Aetolis surgit ab Arpis
Tydides. equidem credo, mea vulnera restant,
30 et tua progenies mortalia demoror arma!
si sine pace tua atque invito numine Troës
Italiam petiere, luant peccata neque illos
iuveris auxilio: sin tot responsa secuti,
quae superi manesque dabant, cur nunc tua quisquam
35 vertere iussa potest? aut cur nova condere fata?
quid repetam exustas Erycino in litore classes?
quid tempestatum regem ventosque furentes
Aeolia excitos aut actam nubibus Irim?
nunc etiam manes – haec intemptata manebat
40 sors rerum – movet, et superis immissa repente
Allecto, medias Italum bacchata per urbes.
nil super imperio moveor; speravimus ista,
dum fortuna fuit; vincant, quos vincere mavis.
si nulla est regio, Teucris quam det tua coniunx
45 dura, per eversae, genitor, fumantia Troiae
excidia obtestor, liceat dimittere ab armis
incolumem Ascanium, liceat superesse nepotem.
Aeneas sane ignotis iactetur in undis,

et, quamcumque viam dederit fortuna, sequatur:
50 hunc tegere et dirae valeam subducere pugnae.
est Amathus, est celsa mihi Paphus atque Cythera
Idaliumque domus: positis inglorius armis
exigat hic aevum. magna dicione iubeto
Karthago premat Ausoniam; nihil urbibus inde
55 obstabit Tyriis. quid pestem evadere belli
iuvit et Argolicos medium fugisse per ignes,
totque maris vastaeque exhausta pericula terrae,
dum Latium Teucri recidivaque Pergama quaerunt?
non satius, cineres patriae insedisse supremos
60 atque solum, quo Troia fuit? Xanthum et Simoënta
redde, oro, miseris, iterumque revolvere casus
da, pater, Iliacos Teucris.'

Juno bitterly reproaches Venus, saying that Turnus and his
Rutulians deserve help just as much as the Trojans.

               tum regia Iuno
acta furore gravi: 'quid me alta silentia cogis
rumpere, et obductum verbis vulgare dolorem?
65 Aenean hominum quisquam divumque subegit
bella sequi, aut hostem regi se inferre Latino?
Italiam petiit fatis auctoribus; esto;
Cassandrae impulsus furiis: num linquere castra
hortati sumus, aut vitam committere ventis?
70 num puero summam belli, num credere muros,
Tyrrhenamve fidem aut gentes agitare quietas?
quis deus in fraudem, quae dura potentia nostra
egit? ubi hic Iuno demissave nubibus Iris?
indignum est, Italos Troiam circumdare flammis
75 nascentem, et patria Turnum consistere terra,

cui Pilumnus avus, cui diva Venilia mater:
quid, face Troianos atra vim ferre Latinis,
arva aliena iugo premere atque avertere praedas?
quid, soceros legere et gremiis abducere pactas,
80   pacem orare manu, praefigere puppibus arma?
tu potes Aenean manibus subducere Graium,
proque viro nebulam et ventos obtendere inanes;
et potes in totidem classem convertere nymphas:
nos aliquid Rutulos contra iuvisse nefandum est?
85   Aeneas ignarus abest: ignarus et absit.
est Paphus Idaliumque tibi, sunt alta Cythera:
quid gravidam bellis urbem et corda aspera temptas?
nosne tibi fluxas Phrygiae res vertere fundo
conamur? nos? an miseros qui Troas Achivis
90   obiecit? quae causa fuit, consurgere in arma
Europamque Asiamque, et foedera solvere furto?
me duce Dardanius Spartam expugnavit adulter?
aut ego tela dedi, fovive cupidine bella?
tum decuit metuisse tuis; nunc sera querelis
95   haud iustis adsurgis et inrite iurgia iactas.'

Jupiter declares that he will support neither side.

    talibus orabat Iuno, cunctique fremebant
caelicolae adsensu vario; ceu flamina prima
cum deprensa fremunt silvis, et caeca volutant
murmura, venturos nautis prodentia ventos.
100   tum pater omnipotens, rerum cui summa potestas,
infit; eo dicente deum domus alta silescit,
et tremefacta solo tellus; silet arduus aether;
tum zephyri posuere; premit placida aequora pontus:

'accipite ergo animis atque haec mea figite dicta.
105 quandoquidem Ausonios coniungi foedere Teucris
haud licitum, nec vestra capit discordia finem:
quae cuique est fortuna hodie, quam quisque secat
    spem,
Tros Rutulusne fuat, nullo discrimine habebo,
seu fatis Italum castra obsidione tenentur,
110 sive errore malo Troiae monitisque sinistris.
nec Rutulos solvo. sua cuique exorsa laborem
fortunamque ferent. rex Iuppiter omnibus idem.
fata viam invenient.' Stygii per flumina fratris,
per pice torrentes atraque voragine ripas
115 adnuit, et totum nutu tremefecit Olympum.
hic finis fandi. solio tum Iuppiter aureo
surgit, caelicolae medium quem ad limina ducunt.

*The Rutulians attack the Trojan camp. Ascanius is
prominent in its defence.*

    interea Rutuli portis circum omnibus instant
sternere caede viros et moenia cingere flammis.
120 at legio Aeneadum vallis obsessa tenetur,
nec spes ulla fugae. miseri stant turribus altis
nequiquam, et rara muros cinxere corona
Asius Imbrasides Hicetaoniusque Thymoetes
Assaracique duo et senior cum Castore Thymbris
125 prima acies; hos germani Sarpedonis ambo
et Clarus et Thaemon, Lycia comitantur ab alta.
fert ingens toto conixus corpore saxum,
haud partem exiguam montis, Lyrnesius Acmon,
nec Clytio genitore minor nec fratre Menestheo.
130 hi iaculis, illi certant defendere saxis,

molirique ignem, nervoque aptare sagittas.
ipse inter medios, Veneris iustissima cura,
Dardanius caput, ecce, puer detectus honestum,
qualis gemma, micat, fulvum quae dividit aurum,
135   aut collo decus aut capiti; vel quale per artem
inclusum buxo aut Oricia terebintho
lucet ebur; fusos cervix cui lactea crines
accipit et molli subnectit circulus auro.
te quoque magnanimae viderunt, Ismare, gentes
140   vulnera derigere et calamos armare veneno,
Maeonia generose domo, ubi pinguia culta
exercentque viri Pactolusque inrigat auro.
adfuit et Mnestheus, quem pulsi pristina Turni
aggere murorum sublimem gloria tollit,
145   et Capys: hinc nomen Campanae ducitur urbi.

Aeneas sails back after forming an alliance with Tarchon.

   illi inter sese duri certamina belli
contulerant: media Aeneas freta nocte secabat.
namque ut ab Euandro castris ingressus Etruscis
regem adit, et regi memorat nomenque genusque;
150   quidve petat, quidve ipse ferat; Mezentius arma
quae sibi conciliet, violentaque pectora Turni
edocet; humanis quae sit fiducia rebus
admonet, immiscetque preces; haud fit mora;
   Tarchon
iungit opes foedusque ferit; tum libera fati
155   classem conscendit iussis gens Lydia divum,
externo commissa duci. Aeneia puppis
prima tenet, rostro Phrygios subiuncta leones;

imminet Ida super, profugis gratissima Teucris.
hic magnus sedet Aeneas, secumque volutat
160 eventus belli varios; Pallasque sinistro
adfixus lateri iam quaerit sidera, opacae
noctis iter, iam quae passus terraque marique.

Tell, Muses, what Etruscan forces accompanied Aeneas.

pandite nunc Helicona, deae, cantusque movete;
quae manus interea Tuscis comitetur ab oris
165 Aenean, armetque rates, pelagoque vehatur.

A list of the Etruscan chiefs including Ocnus, founder of Mantua.

Massicus aerata princeps secat aequora Tigri:
sub quo mille manus iuvenum, qui moenia Clusi
quique urbem liquere Cosas; quis tela sagittae
gorytique leves umeris et letifer arcus.
170 una torvus Abas; huic totum insignibus armis
agmen et aurato fulgebat Apolline puppis.
sescentos illi dederat Populonia mater
expertos belli iuvenes; ast Ilva trecentos
insula inexhaustis Chalybum generosa metallis.
175 tertius, ille hominum divumque interpres Asilas,
cui pecudum fibrae, caeli cui sidera parent
et linguae volucrum et praesagi fulminis ignes,
mille rapit densos acie atque horrentibus hastis.
hos parere iubent Alpheae ab origine Pisae,
180 urbs Etrusca solo. sequitur pulcherrimus Astur,
Astur equo fidens et versicoloribus armis.
ter centum adiciunt, – mens omnibus una sequendi -
qui Caerete domo, qui sunt Minionis in arvis,

et Pyrgi veteres intempestaeque Graviscae.

185   non ego te, Ligurum ductor fortissime bello,
transierim, Cinyre, et paucis comitate Cupavo,
cuius olorinae surgunt de vertice pinnae -
crimen, Amor, vestrum – formaeque insigne paternae.
namque ferunt luctu Cycnum Phaëthontis amati,

190   populeas inter frondes umbramque sororum
dum canit, et maestum musa solatur amorem,
canentem molli pluma duxisse senectam,
linquentem terras et sidera voce sequentem.
filius, aequales comitatus classe catervas,

195   ingentem remis Centaurum promovet; ille
instat aquae saxumque undis immane minatur
arduus, et longa sulcat maria alta carina.
      ille etiam patriis agmen ciet Ocnus ab oris,
fatidicae Mantus et Tusci filius amnis,

200   qui muros matrisque dedit tibi, Mantua, nomen,
Mantua, dives avis; sed non genus omnibus unum:
gens illi triplex, populi sub gente quaterni;
ipsa caput populis; Tusco de sanguine vires.
hinc quoque quingentos in se Mezentius armat,

205   quos patre Benaco velatus harundine glauca
Mincius infesta ducebat in aequora pinu.
it gravis Aulestes, centenaque arbore fluctum
verberat adsurgens; spumant vada marmore verso.
hunc vehit immanis Triton et caerula concha

210   exterrens freta; cui laterum tenus hispida nanti
frons hominem praefert, in pristim desinit alvus;
spumea semifero sub pectore murmurat unda.
tot lecti proceres ter denis navibus ibant

subsidio Troiae, et campos salis aere secabant.

Sea nymphs urge Aeneas to relieve the Trojan camp. Sighting it, Aeneas raises his shield on high and is greeted by a cheer from the besieged.

215   iamque dies caelo concesserat, almaque curru
noctivago Phoebe medium pulsabat Olympum:
Aeneas – neque enim membris dat cura quietem -
ipse sedens clavumque regit velisque ministrat;
atque illi medio in spatio chorus, ecce, suarum
220 occurrit comitum; nymphae, quas alma Cybebe
numen habere maris nymphasque e navibus esse
iusserat, innabant pariter fluctusque secabant,
quot prius aeratae steterant ad litora prorae.
agnoscunt longe regem, lustrantque choreis.
225 quarum quae fandi doctissima Cymodocea,
pone sequens dextra puppim tenet, ipsaque dorso
eminet, ac laeva tacitis subremigat undis.
tum sic ignarum adloquitur: 'vigilasne, deum gens,
Aenea? vigila, et velis immitte rudentes.
230 nos sumus, Idaeae sacro de vertice pinus,
nunc pelagi nymphae, classis tua. perfidus ut nos
praecipites ferro Rutulus flammaque premebat,
rupimus invitae tua vincula, teque per aequor
quaerimus. hanc genetrix faciem miserata refecit,
235 et dedit esse deas, aevumque agitare sub undis.
at puer Ascanius muro fossisque tenetur
tela inter media atque horrentes Marte Latinos.
iam loca iussa tenet forti permixtus Etrusco
Arcas eques. medias illis opponere turmas
240 ne castris iungant, certa est sententia Turno.

surge age, et Aurora socios veniente vocari
primus in arma iube, et clipeum cape, quem dedit ipse
invictum ignipotens, atque oras ambiit auro.
crastina lux, mea si non inrita dicta putaris,
245 ingentes Rutulae spectabit caedis acervos.'
dixerat: et dextra discedens impulit altam,
haud ignara modi, puppim. fugit illa per undas
ocior et iaculo et ventos aequante sagitta.
inde aliae celerant cursus. stupet inscius ipse
250 Tros Anchisiades; animos tamen omine tollit.
tum breviter supera aspectans convexa precatur:
'alma parens Idaea deum, cui Dindyma cordi,
turrigeraeque urbes biiugique ad frena leones;
tu mihi nunc pugnae princeps, tu rite propinques
255 augurium, Phrygibusque adsis pede, diva, secundo.'
tantum effatus; et interea revoluta ruebat
matura iam luce dies, noctemque fugarat.
principio sociis edicit, signa sequantur,
atque animos aptent armis, pugnaeque parent se.
260   iamque in conspectu Teucros habet et sua castra,
stans celsa in puppi, clipeum cum deinde sinistra
extulit ardentem. clamorem ad sidera tollunt
Dardanidae e muris; spes addita suscitat iras;
tela manu iaciunt; quales sub nubibus atris
265 Strymoniae dant signa grues, atque aethera tranant
cum sonitu, fugiuntque notos clamore secundo.
at Rutulo regi ducibusque ea mira videri
Ausoniis, donec versas ad litora puppes
respiciunt, totumque adlabi classibus aequor.
270 ardet apex capiti, cristisque a vertice flamma

funditur, et vastos umbo vomit aureus ignes:
non secus ac liquida si quando nocte cometae
sanguinei lugubre rubent, aut Sirius ardor
ille sitim morbosque ferens mortalibus aegris
275   nascitur, et laevo contristat lumine caelum.

*Turnus is not dismayed. He inspires his men to attack the
Trojans while they are engaged in landing.*

haud tamen audaci Turno fiducia cessit
litora praecipere, et venientes pellere terra.
[ultro animos tollit dictis, atque increpat ultro:]
'quod votis optastis, adest, perfringere dextra.
280   in manibus Mars ipse, viri. nunc coniugis esto
quisque suae tectique memor; nunc magna referto
facta, patrum laudes. ultro occurramus ad undam,
dum trepidi, egressisque labant vestigia prima.
audentes fortuna iuvat.'
285   haec ait, et secum versat, quos ducere contra,
vel quibus obsessos possit concredere muros.

*Aeneas' forces land. Tarchon runs his ships ashore but his
own ship is broken up by the surf.*

interea Aeneas socios de puppibus altis
pontibus exponit. multi servare recursus
languentis pelagi, et brevibus se credere saltu;
290   per remos alii. speculatus litora Tarchon,
qua vada non spirant nec fracta remurmurat unda,
sed mare inoffensum crescenti adlabitur aestu,
advertit subito proram, sociosque precatur:
'nunc, o lecta manus, validis incumbite remis;
295   tollite, ferte rates; inimicam findite rostris

hanc terram, sulcumque sibi premat ipsa carina.
frangere nec tali puppim statione recuso,
arrepta tellure semel.' quae talia postquam
effatus Tarchon, socii consurgere tonsis
300   spumantesque rates arvis inferre Latinis,
donec rostra tenent siccum et sedere carinae
omnes innocuae. sed non puppis tua, Tarchon.
namque, inflicta vadis, dorso dum pendet iniquo
anceps sustentata diu, fluctusque fatigat,
305   solvitur, atque viros mediis exponit in undis;
fragmina remorum quos et fluitantia transtra
impediunt, retrahitque pedes simul unda relabens.

*The fight begins. Aeneas kills many of the enemy but Clausus
claims many victims also. The battle continues fiercely.*

    nec Turnum segnis retinet mora; sed rapit acer
totam aciem in Teucros, et contra in litore sistit.
310   signa canunt. primus turmas invasit agrestes
Aeneas, omen pugnae, stravitque Latinos,
occiso Therone, virum qui maximus ultro
Aenean petit: huic gladio perque aerea suta,
per tunicam squalentem auro, latus haurit apertum.
315   inde Lichan ferit, exsectum iam matre perempta,
et tibi, Phoebe, sacrum, casus evadere ferri
quod licuit parvo. nec longe, Cissea durum
immanemque Gyan, sternentes agmina clava,
deiecit leto; nihil illos Herculis arma,
320   nec validae iuvere manus genitorque Melampus,
Alcidae comes usque, graves dum terra labores
praebuit. ecce Pharo, voces dum iactat inertes,
intorquens iaculum clamanti sistit in ore.

tu quoque, flaventem prima lanugine malas
325 dum sequeris Clytium infelix, nova gaudia, Cydon,
Dardania stratus dextra, securus amorum,
qui iuvenum tibi semper erant, miserande, iaceres,
ni fratrum stipata cohors foret obvia, Phorci
progenies, septem numero, septenaque tela
330 coniciunt; partim galea clipeoque resultant
inrita, deflexit partim stringentia corpus
alma Venus. fidum Aeneas adfatur Achaten:
'suggere tela mihi; non ullum dextera frustra
torserit in Rutulos, steterunt quae in corpore Graium
335 Iliacis campis.' tum magnam corripit hastam,
et iacit; illa volans clipei transverberat aera
Maeonis, et thoraca simul cum pectore rumpit.
huic frater subit Alcanor, fratremque ruentem
sustentat dextra: traiecto missa lacerto
340 protinus hasta fugit servatque cruenta tenorem,
dexteraque ex umero nervis moribunda pependit.
tum Numitor, iaculo fratris de corpore rapto,
Aenean petiit; sed non et figere contra
est licitum, magnique femur perstrinxit Achatae.
345 hic Curibus, fidens primaevo corpore, Clausus
advenit, et rigida Dryopem ferit eminus hasta
sub mentum, graviter pressa, pariterque loquentis
vocem animamque rapit traiecto gutture; at ille
fronte ferit terram, et crassum vomit ore cruorem.
350 tres quoque Threïcios Boreae de gente suprema,
et tres, quos Idas pater et patria Ismara mittit,
per varios sternit casus. accurrit Halaesus,
Auruncaeque manus; subit et Neptunia proles,

insignis Messapus equis. expellere tendunt
355   nunc hi, nunc illi; certatur limine in ipso
Ausoniae. magno discordes aethere venti
proelia ceu tollunt animis et viribus aequis;
non ipsi inter se, non nubila, non mare cedit;
anceps pugna diu; stant obnixa omnia contra:
360   haud aliter Troianae acies aciesque Latinae
concurrunt; haeret pede pes densusque viro vir.

*The Arcadian cavalry retreat but are rallied by Pallas who
wreaks havoc among the enemy killing the formidable
Halaesus.*

   at parte ex alia, qua saxa rotantia late
impulerat torrens arbustaque diruta ripis,
Arcadas, insuetos acies inferre pedestres,
365   ut vidit Pallas Latio dare terga sequaci -
aspera quis natura loci dimittere quando
suasit equos – unum quod rebus restat egenis,
nunc prece, nunc dictis virtutem accendit amaris:
'quo fugitis, socii? per vos et fortia facta,
370   per ducis Euandri nomen devictaque bella,
spemque meam, patriae quae nunc subit aemula laudi,
fidite ne pedibus. ferro rumpenda per hostes
est via. qua globus ille virum densissimus urget,
hac vos et Pallanta ducem patria alta reposcit.
375   numina nulla premunt; mortali urgemur ab hoste
mortales; totidem nobis animaeque manusque.
ecce, maris magna claudit nos obice pontus;
deest iam terra fugae. pelagus Troiamque petemus?'
haec ait, et medius densos prorumpit in hostes.
380   obvius huic primum, fatis adductus iniquis,

fit Lagus; hunc, magno vellit dum pondere saxum,
intorto figit telo, discrimina costis
per medium qua spina dabat; hastamque receptat
ossibus haerentem. quem non super occupat Hisbo
385   ille quidem hoc sperans; nam Pallas ante ruentem
dum furit, incautum crudeli morte sodalis,
excipit, atque ensem tumido in pulmone recondit.
hinc Sthenelum petit, et Rhoeti de gente vetusta
Anchemolum, thalamos ausum incestare novercae.
390   vos etiam gemini Rutulis cecidistis in arvis,
Daucia, Laride Thymberque, simillima proles,
indiscreta suis gratusque parentibus error;
at nunc dura dedit vobis discrimina Pallas:
nam tibi, Thymbre, caput Euandrius abstulit ensis;
395   te decisa suum, Laride, dextera quaerit,
semianimesque micant digiti ferrumque retractant.
Arcadas, accensos monitu et praeclara tuentes
facta viri, mixtus dolor et pudor armat in hostes.
tum Pallas biiugis fugientem Rhoetea praeter
400   traicit. hoc spatium tantumque morae fuit Ilo;
Ilo namque procul validam derexerat hastam:
quam medius Rhoeteus intercipit, optime Teuthra,
te fugiens, fratremque Tyren; curruque volutus
caedit semianimis Rutulorum calcibus arva.
405   ac velut, optato ventis aestate coortis,
dispersa immittit silvis incendia pastor;
correptis subito mediis extenditur una
horrida per latos acies Volcania campos;
ille sedens victor flammas despectat ovantes:
410   non aliter socium virtus coit omnis in unum,

teque iuvat, Palla. sed bellis acer Halaesus
tendit in adversos, seque in sua colligit arma.
hic mactat Ladona Pheretaque Demodocumque;
Strymonio dextram fulgenti deripit ense
415   elatam in iugulum; saxo ferit ora Thoantis,
ossaque dispersit cerebro permixta cruento.
fata canens silvis genitor celarat Halaesum;
ut senior leto canentia lumina solvit,
iniecere manum Parcae, telisque sacrarunt
420   Euandri. quem sic Pallas petit ante precatus:
'da nunc, Thybri pater, ferro, quod missile libro,
fortunam atque viam duri per pectus Halaesi:
haec arma exuviasque viri tua quercus habebit.'
audiit illa deus; dum texit Imaona Halaesus,
425   Arcadio infelix telo dat pectus inermum.
at non caede viri tanta perterrita Lausus,
pars ingens belli, sinit agmina: primus Abantem
oppositum interimit, pugnae nodumque moramque.
sternitur Arcadiae proles, sternuntur Etrusci,
430   et vos, o Grais imperdita corpora, Teucri.
agmina concurrunt ducibusque et viribus aequis.
extremi addensent acies; nec turba moveri
tela manusque sinit. hinc Pallas instat et urget,
hinc contra Lausus – nec multum discrepat aetas -
435   egregii forma, sed quis fortuna negarat
in patriam reditus. ipsos concurrere passus
haud tamen inter se magni regnator Olympi:
mox illos sua fata manent maiore sub hoste.

Turnus meets Pallas and slays him. Turnus exults and removes Pallas' golden belt, an action which is later to seal his fate.

    interea soror alma monet succedere Lauso

440 Turnum, qui volucri curru medium secat agmen.

ut vidit socios: 'tempus desistere pugnae;

solus ego in Pallanta feror; soli mihi Pallas

debetur; cuperem ipse parens spectator adesset.'

haec ait; et socii cesserunt aequore iusso.

445 at, Rutulum abscessu, iuvenis tum iussa superba

miratus stupet in Turno, corpusque per ingens

lumina volvit, obitque truci procul omnia visu,

talibus et dictis it contra dicta tyranni:

'aut spoliis ego iam raptis laudabor opimis,

450 aut leto insigni; sorti pater aequus utrique est.

tolle minas.' fatus medium procedit in aequor.

frigidus Arcadibus coit in praecordia sanguis.

desiluit Turnus biiugis; pedes apparat ire

comminus. utque leo, specula cum vidit ab alta

455 stare procul campis meditantem in proelia

      taurum,

advolat, haud alia est Turni venientis imago.

hunc ubi contiguum missae fore credidit hastae,

ire prior Pallas, si qua fors adiuvet ausum

viribus imparibus, magnumque ita ad aethera fatur:

460 'per patris hospitium et mensas, quas advena adisti,

te precor, Alcide, coeptis ingentibus adsis.

cernat semineci sibi me rapere arma cruenta,

victoremque ferant morientia lumina Turni.'

audiit Alcides iuvenem, magnumque sub imo

465 corde premit gemitum lacrimasque effundit inanes.

tum genitor natum dictis adfatur amicis:
'stat sua cuique dies; breve et inreparabile tempus
omnibus est vitae; sed famam extendere factis,
hoc virtutis opus. Troiae sub moenibus altis
470   tot nati cecidere deum; quin occidit una
Sarpedon, mea progenies. etiam sua Turnum
fata vocant, metasque dati pervenit ad aevi.'
sic ait, atque oculos Rutulorum reicit arvis.
    at Pallas magnis emittit viribus hastam,
475   vaginaque cava fulgentem deripit ensem.
illa volans, umeri surgunt qua tegmina summa,
incidit, atque, viam clipei molita per oras,
tandem etiam magno strinxit de corpore Turni.
hic Turnus ferro praefixum robur acuto
480   in Pallanta diu librans iacit, atque ita fatur:
'aspice, num mage sit nostrum penetrabile telum.'
dixerat; at clipeum, tot ferri terga, tot aeris,
quem pellis totiens obeat circumdata tauri,
vibranti medium cuspis transverberat ictu,
485   loricaeque moras et pectus perforat ingens.
ille rapit calidum frustra de vulnere telum:
una eademque via sanguis animusque sequuntur.
corruit in vulnus; sonitum super arma dedere;
et terram hostilem moriens petit ore cruento.
490   quem Turnus super adsistens:
'Arcades, haec' inquit 'memores mea dicta referte
Euandro: qualem meruit, Pallanta remitto.
quisquis honos tumuli, quidquid solamen humandi
    est,
largior: haud illi stabunt Aeneïa parvo

495 hospitia.' et laevo pressit pede, talia fatus,
     exanimem, rapiens immania pondera baltei,
     impressumque nefas: una sub nocte iugali
     caesa manus iuvenum foede, thalamique cruenti,
     quae Clonus Eurytides multo caelaverat auro:
500 quo nunc Turnus ovat spolio gaudetque potitus.
     nescia mens hominum fati sortisque futurae,
     et servare modum, rebus sublata secundis!
     Turno tempus erit, magno cum optaverit emptum
     intactum Pallanta, et cum spolia ista diemque
505 oderit. at socii multo gemitu lacrimisque
     impositum scuto referunt Pallanta frequentes.
     o dolor atque decus magnum rediture parenti!
     haec te prima dies bello dedit, haec eadem aufert,
     cum tamen ingentes Rutulorum linquis acervos!

Aeneas hews his way through the enemy, slaying a host of warriors. He reaches the Trojan camp and relieves the siege.

510   nec iam fama mali tanti, sed certior auctor
     advolat Aeneae, tenui discrimine leti
     esse suos; tempus, versis succurrere Teucris.
     proxima quaeque metit gladio, latumque per agmen
     ardens limitem agit ferro, te, Turne, superbum
515 caede nova quaerens. Pallas, Euander, in ipsis
     omnia sunt oculis, mensae, quas advena primas
     tunc adiit, dextraeque datae. Sulmone creatos
     quattuor hic iuvenes, totidem, quos educat Ufens,
     viventes rapit, inferias quos immolet umbris,
520 captivoque rogi perfundat sanguine flammas.
     inde Mago procul infensam contenderat hastam.
     ille astu subit; at tremibunda supervolat hasta;

et genua amplectens effatur talia supplex:
'per patrios manes et spes surgentis Iuli
525   te precor, hanc animam serves natoque patrique.
est domus alta; iacent penitus defossa talenta
caelati argenti; sunt auri pondera facti
infectique mihi. non hic victoria Teucrum
vertitur, aut anima una dabit discrimina tanta.'
530   dixerat. Aeneas contra cui talia reddit:
'argenti atque auri memoras quae multa talenta,
natis parce tuis. belli commercia Turnus
sustulit ista prior iam tum Pallante perempto.
hoc patris Anchisae manes, hoc sentit Iulus.'
535   sic fatus galeam laeva tenet, atque reflexa
cervice orantis capulo tenus applicat ensem.
nec procul Haemonides, Phoebi Triviaeque sacerdos,
infula cui sacra redimibat tempora vitta,
totus conlucens veste atque insignibus albis;
540   quem congressus agit campo, lapsumque superstans
immolat, ingentique umbra tegit; arma Serestus
lecta refert umeris, tibi, rex Gradive, tropaeum.
     instaurant acies Volcani stirpe creatus
Caeculus et veniens Marsorum montibus Umbro.
545   Dardanides contra furit. Anxuris ense sinistram
et totum clipei ferro deiecerat orbem; -
dixerat ille aliquid magnum, vimque adfore verbo
crediderat, caeloque animum fortasse ferebat,
canitiemque sibi et longos promiserat annos; -
550   Tarquitus exsultans contra fulgentibus armis,
silvicolae Fauno Dryope quem nympha crearat,
obvius ardenti sese obtulit. ille reducta

loricam clipeique ingens onus impedit hasta;
tum caput orantis nequiquam et multa **parantis**
555   dicere deturbat terrae, truncumque tepentem
provolvens super haec inimico pectore fatur:
'istic nunc, metuende, iace! non te optima mater
condet humi, patrioque onerabit membra sepulchro:
alitibus linquere feris, aut gurgite mersum
560   unda feret, piscesque impasti vulnera lambent.'
protinus Antaeum et Lucam, prima agmina Turni,
persequitur, fortemque Numam, fulvumque Camer-
    tem,
magnanimo Volcente satum, ditissimus agri
qui fuit Ausonidum, et tacitis regnavit Amyclis.
565   Aegaeon qualis, centum cui bracchia dicunt
centenasque manus, quinquaginta oribus ignem
pectoribusque arsisse, Iovis cum fulmina contra
tot paribus streperet clipeis, tot stringeret enses:
sic toto Aeneas desaevit in aequore victor,
570   ut semel intepuit mucro. quin ecce Niphaei
quadriiuges in equos adversaque pectora tendit
atque illi, longe gradientem et dira frementem
ut videre, metu versi retroque ruentes
effunduntque ducem, rapiuntque ad litora currus.
575   interea biiugis infert se Lucagus albis
in medios, fraterque Liger; sed frater habenis
flectit equos, strictum rotat acer Lucagus ensem.
haud tulit Aeneas tanto fervore furentes:
inruit, adversaque ingens apparuit hasta.
580   cui Liger:
'non Diomedis equos, nec currum cernis Achilli,

aut Phrygiae campos; nunc belli finis et aevi
his dabitur terris.' vesano talia late
dicta volant Ligeri; sed non et Troïus heros
585 dicta parat contra; iaculum nam torquet in hostem.
Lucagus ut pronus pendens in verbera telo
admonuit biiugos, proiecto dum pede laevo
aptat se pugnae, subit oras hasta per imas
fulgentis clipei, tum laevum perforat inguen;
590 excussus curru moribundus volvitur arvis.
quem pius Aeneas dictis adfatur amaris:
'Lucage, nulla tuos currus fuga segnis equorum
prodidit, aut vanae vertere ex hostibus umbrae;
ipse rotis saliens iuga deseris.' haec ita fatus
595 arripuit biiugos; frater tendebat inertes
infelix palmas, curru delapsus eodem:
'per te, per qui te talem genuere parentes,
vir Troiane, sine hanc animam, et miserere precantis.'
pluribus oranti Aeneas: 'haud talia dudum
600 dicta dabas. morere, et fratrem ne desere frater.'
tum, latebras animae, pectus mucrone recludit.
talia per campos edebat funera ductor
Dardanius, torrentis aquae vel turbinis atri
more furens. tandem erumpunt et castra relinquunt
605 Ascanius puer et nequiquam obsessa iuventus.

*Juno is allowed to delay Turnus' fate. She makes a phantom
in the likeness of Aeneas. It boards a ship and, when Turnus
follows, disappears. Juno sets the ship adrift; Turnus is only
prevented by Juno from committing suicide.*

Iunonem interea compellat Iuppiter ultro:
'o germana mihi atque eadem gratissima coniunx,

ut rebare, Venus – nec te sententia fallit –
Troianas sustentat opes, non vivida bello
610 dextra viris animusque ferox patiensque pericli.'
cui Iuno summissa: 'quid, o pulcherrime coniunx,
sollicitas aegram et tua tristia dicta timentem?
si mihi, quae quondam fuerat, quamque esse decebat,
vis in amore foret, non hoc mihi namque negares,
615 omnipotens, quin et pugnae subducere Turnum,
et Dauno possem incolumem servare parenti.
nunc pereat, Teucrisque pio det sanguine poenas.
ille tamen nostra deducit origine nomen,
Pilumnusque illi quartus pater; et tua larga
620 saepe manu multisque oneravit limina donis.'
cui rex aetherii breviter sic fatur Olympi:
'si mora praesentis leti tempusque caduco
oratur iuveni, meque hoc ita ponere sentis,
tolle fuga Turnum atque instantibus eripe fatis.
625 hactenus indulsisse vacat. sin altior istis
sub precibus venia ulla latet, totumque moveri
mutarive putas bellum, spes pascis inanes.'
et Iuno adlacrimans: 'quid si, quae voce gravaris,
mente dares, atque haec Turno rata vita maneret?
630 nunc manet insontem gravis exitus; aut ego veri
vana feror. quod ut o potius formidine falsa
ludar, et in melius tua, qui potes, orsa reflectas!'
    haec ubi dicta dedit, caelo se protinus alto
misit, agens hiemem, nimbo succincta, per auras,
635 Iliacamque aciem et Laurentia castra petivit.
tum dea nube cava tenuem sine viribus umbram
in faciem Aeneae, visu mirabile monstrum,

Dardaniis ornat telis, clipeumque iubasque
divini adsimulat capitis; dat inania verba;
640 dat sine mente sonum, gressusque effingit euntis:
morte obita quales fama est volitare figuras,
aut quae sopitos deludunt somnia sensus.
at primas laeta ante acies exsultat imago,
inritatque virum telis et voce lacessit.
645 instat cui Turnus, stridentemque eminus hastam
conicit; illa dato vertit vestigia tergo.
tum vero Aenean aversum ut cedere Turnus
credidit, atque animo spem turbidus hausit inanem:
'quo fugis, Aenea? thalamos ne desere pactos;
650 hac dabitur dextra tellus quaesita per undas.'
talia vociferans sequitur, strictumque coruscat
mucronem; nec ferre videt sua gaudia ventos.
      forte ratis celsi coniuncta crepidine saxi
expositis stabat scalis et ponte parato,
655 qua rex Clusinis advectus Osinius oris.
huc sese trepida Aeneae fugientis imago
conicit in latebras; nec Turnus segnior instat,
exsuperatque moras, et pontes transilit altos.
vix proram attigerat: rumpit Saturnia funem,
660 avulsamque rapit revoluta per aequora navem.
illum autem Aeneas absentem in proelia poscit;
obvia multa virum demittit corpora morti.
tum levis haud ultra latebras iam quaerit imago,
sed sublime volans nubi se immiscuit atrae,
665 cum Turnum medio interea fert aequore turbo.
respicit ignarus rerum ingratusque salutis,
et duplices cum voce manus ad sidera tendit:

'omnipotens genitor, tanton me crimine dignum
duxisti, et tales voluisti expendere poenas?
670 quo feror? unde abii? quae me fuga, quemve reducit?
Laurentesne iterum muros aut castra videbo?
quid manus illa virum, qui me meaque arma secuti?
quosne, nefas, omnes infanda in morte reliqui,
et nunc palantes video, gemitumque cadentum
675 accipio? quid ago? aut quae iam satis ima dehiscat
terra mihi? vos o potius miserescite, venti;
in rupes, in saxa – volens vos Turnus adoro –
ferte ratem, saevisque vadis immittite Syrtis,
quo neque me Rutuli, nec conscia fama sequatur.'
680 haec memorans, animo nunc huc, nunc fluctuat illuc,
an sese mucrone ob tantum dedecus amens
induat, et crudum per costas exigat ensem;
fluctibus an iaciat mediis, et litora nando
curva petat, Teucrumque iterum se reddat in arma.
685 ter conatus utramque viam; ter maxima Iuno
continuit, iuvenemque animi miserata repressit.
labitur alta secans fluctuque aestuque secundo,
et patris antiquam Dauni defertur ad urbem.

*Mezentius joins the battle and holds his ground against all
attacks. He kills many but is warned of his own approaching
death.*

    at Iovis interea monitis Mezentius ardens
690 succedit pugnae, Teucrosque invadit ovantes.
concurrunt Tyrrhenae acies, atque omnibus uni,
uni odiisque viro telisque frequentibus instant.
ille, velut rupes, vastum quae prodit in aequor,
obvia ventorum furiis expostaque ponto,

695 vim cunctam atque minas perfert caelique marisque,
ipsa immota manens, prolem Dolichaonis Hebrum
sternit humi; cum quo Latagum Palmumque fugacem,
sed Latagum saxo atque ingenti fragmine montis
occupat os faciemque adversam; poplite Palmum
700 succiso volvi segnem sinit; armaque Lauso
donat habere umeris et vertice figere cristas.
nec non Euanthen Phrygium, Paridisque Mimanta
aequalem comitemque; una quem nocte Theano
in lucem genitori Amyco dedit, et face praegnans
705 Cisseïs regina Parim; Paris urbe paterna
occubat; ignarum Laurens habet ora Mimanta.
ac velut ille canum morsu de montibus altis
actus aper, multos Vesulus quem pinifer annos
defendit, multosque palus Laurentia, silva
710 pastus harundinea, postquam inter retia ventum est,
substitit, infremuitque ferox, et inhorruit armos;
nec cuiquam irasci propiusque accedere virtus,
sed iaculis tutisque procul clamoribus instant:
haud aliter, iustae quibus est Mezentius irae,
715 non ulli est animus stricto concurrere ferro;
missilibus longe et vasto clamore lacessunt:
ille autem impavidus partes cunctatur in omnes,
dentibus infrendens, et tergo decutit hastas.
        venerat antiquis Corythi de finibus Acron,
720 Graius homo, infectos linquens profugus hymenaeos;
hunc ubi miscentem longe media agmina vidit,
purpureum pinnis et pactae coniugis ostro:
impastus stabula alta leo ceu saepe peragrans -
suadet enim vesana fames – si forte fugacem

725 conspexit capream aut surgentem in cornua cervum,
gaudet, hians immane, comasque arrexit, et haeret
visceribus super incumbens; lavit improba taeter
ora cruor:
sic ruit in densos alacer Mezentius hostes.
730 sternitur infelix Acron, et calcibus atram
tundit humum exspirans, infractaque tela cruentat.
atque idem fugientem haud est dignatus Oroden
sternere, nec iacta caecum dare cuspide vulnus;
obvius adversoque occurrit, seque viro vir
735 contulit, haud furto melior sed fortibus armis.
tum super abiectum posito pede nixus et hasta:
'pars belli haud temnenda, viri, iacet altus Orodes.'
conclamant socii laetum paeana secuti.
ille autem exspirans: 'non me, quicumque es, inulto,
740 victor, nec longum laetabere; te quoque fata
prospectant paria, atque eadem mox arva tenebis.'
ad quae subridens mixta Mezentius ira:
'nunc morere: ast de me divum pater atque hominum
rex
viderit.' hoc dicens eduxit corpore telum;
745 olli dura quies oculos et ferreus urget
somnus; in aeternam clauduntur lumina noctem.

As the battle rages Aeneas and Mezentius meet. The wounded Mezentius is saved by his son Lausus and carried off the battlefield. Aeneas kills Lausus but pities his fatal devotion to his father.

    Caedicus Alcathoum obtruncat, Sacrator Hydaspen,
Partheniumque Rapo et praedurum viribus Orsen,
Messapus Cloniumque Lycaoniumque Ericaeten,

750 illum infrenis equi lapsu tellure iacentem,
hunc peditem. pedes et Lycius processerat Agis;
quem tamen haud expers Valerus virtutis avitae
deicit; at Thronium Salius, Saliumque Nealces,
insignis iaculo et longe fallente sagitta.
755   iam gravis aequabat luctus et mutua Mavors
funera, caedebant pariter pariterque ruebant
victores victique; neque his fuga nota neque illis.
di Iovis in tectis iram miserantur inanem
amborum, et tantos mortalibus esse labores;
760 hinc Venus, hinc contra spectat Saturnia Iuno:
pallida Tisiphone media inter milia saevit.
at vero ingentem quatiens Mezentius hastam
turbidus ingreditur campo. quam magnus Orion,
cum pedes incedit medii per maxima Nerei
765 stagna viam scindens, umero supereminet undas,
aut, summis referens annosam montibus ornum,
ingrediturque solo et caput inter nubila condit:
talis se vastis infert Mezentius armis.
    huic contra Aeneas, speculatus in agmine longo,
770 obvius ire parat. manet imperterritus ille,
hostem magnanimum opperiens, et mole sua stat;
atque oculis spatium emensus, quantum satis hastae:
'dextra mihi deus et telum, quod missile libro,
nunc adsint: voveo praedonis corpore raptis
775 indutum spoliis ipsum te, Lause, tropaeum
Aeneae.' dixit, stridentemque eminus hastam
iecit; at illa volans clipeo est excussa, proculque
egregium Antoren latus inter et ilia figit,
Herculis Antoren comitem, qui missus ab Argis

780 haeserat Euandro, atque Itala consederat urbe.
     sternitur infelix alieno vulnere, caelumque
     aspicit, et dulces moriens reminiscitur Argos.
     tum pius Aeneas hastam iacit; illa per orbem
     aere cavum triplici, per linea terga, tribusque
785 transiit intextum tauris opus, imaque sedit
     inguine; sed vires haud pertulit. ocius ensem
     Aeneas, viso Tyrrheni sanguine laetus,
     eripit a femine et trepidanti fervidus instat.
     ingemuit cari graviter genitoris amore,
790 ut vidit, Lausus; lacrimaeque per ora volutae.
          hic mortis durae casum tuaque optima facta,
     si qua fidem tanto est operi latura vetustas,
     non equidem, nec te, iuvenis memorande, silebo.
          ille pedem referens et inutilis inque ligatus
795 cedebat, clipeoque inimicum hastile trahebat.
     prorupit iuvenis seseque immiscuit armis;
     iamque adsurgentis dextra plagamque ferentis
     Aeneae subiit mucronem, ipsumque morando
     sustinuit; socii magno clamore sequuntur,
800 dum genitor nati parma·protectus abiret;
     telaque coniciunt, proturbantque eminus hostem
     missilibus. furit Aeneas, tectusque tenet se.
     ac velut effusa si quando grandine nimbi
     praecipitant, omnis campis diffugit arator,
805 omnis et agricola, et tuta latet arce viator,
     aut amnis ripis, aut alti fornice saxi,
     dum pluit in terris, ut possint sole reducto
     exercere diem: sic obrutus undique telis
     Aeneas nubem belli, dum detonet omnis,

810 sustinet, et Lausum increpitat Lausoque minatur:
'quo moriture ruis, maioraque viribus audes?
fallit te incautum pietas tua.' nec minus ille
exsultat demens. saevae iamque altius irae
Dardanio surgunt ductori, extremaque Lauso
815 Parcae fila legunt: validum namque exigit ensem
per medium Aeneas iuvenem, totumque recondit.
transiit et parmam mucro, levia arma minacis,
et tunicam, molli mater quam neverat auro,
implevitque sinum sanguis; tum vita per auras
820 concessit maesta ad manes corpusque reliquit.
at vero ut vultum vidit morientis et ora,
ora modis Anchisiades pallentia miris,
ingemuit miserans graviter dextramque tetendit,
et mentem patriae subiit pietatis imago.
825 'quid tibi nunc, miserande puer, pro laudibus istis,
quid pius Aeneas tanta dabit indole dignum?
arma, quibus laetatus, habe tua; teque parentum
manibus et cineri, si qua est ea cura, remitto.
hoc tamen infelix miseram solabere mortem:
830 Aeneae magni dextra cadis.' increpat ultro
cunctantes socios, et terra sublevat ipsum
sanguine turpantem comptos de more capillos.

Mezentius hearing of his son's death mounts his horse and rides to confront Aeneas. He vainly showers Aeneas with javelins; Aeneas pierces the head of Mezentius' horse with a spear and stands over Mezentius as he lies pinned to the ground. Mezentius seeks no pity but asks to be buried with his son.

interea genitor Tiberini ad fluminis undam
vulnera siccabat lymphis, corpusque levabat

835 arboris adclinis trunco. procul aerea ramis
dependet galea et prato gravia arma quiescunt.
stant lecti circum iuvenes; ipse aeger, anhelans,
colla fovet, fusus propexam in pectore barbam;
multa super Lauso rogitat, multumque remittit,

840 qui revocent, maestique ferant mandata parentis.
at Lausum socii exanimem super arma ferebant
flentes, ingentem atque ingenti vulnere victum.
agnovit longe gemitum praesaga mali mens.
canitiem multo deformat pulvere, et ambas

845 ad caelum tendit palmas, et corpore inhaeret.
'tantane me tenuit vivendi, nate, voluptas,
ut pro me hostili paterer succedere dextrae,
quem genui? tuane haec genitor per vulnera servor,
morte tua vivens? heu, nunc misero mihi demum

850 exsilium infelix! nunc alte vulnus adactum!
idem ego, nate, tuum maculavi crimine nomen,
pulsus ob invidiam solio sceptrisque paternis.
debueram patriae poenas odiisque meorum:
omnes per mortes animam sontem ipse dedissem.

855 nunc vivo, neque adhuc homines lucemque relinquo:
sed linquam.' simul hoc dicens attollit in aegrum
se femur, et, quamquam vis alto vulnere tardat,
haud deiectus equum duci iubet. hoc decus illi,
hoc solamen erat; bellis hoc victor abibat

860 omnibus. adloquitur maerentem, et talibus infit:
'Rhaebe, diu, res si qua diu mortalibus ulla est,
viximus. aut hodie victor spolia illa cruenta
et caput Aeneae referes, Lausique dolorum
ultor eris mecum, aut, aperit si nulla viam vis,

865 occumbes pariter. neque enim, fortissime, credo,
iussa aliena pati et dominos dignabere Teucros.'
dixit, et exceptus tergo consueta locavit
membra, manusque ambas iaculis oneravit acutis,
aere caput fulgens, cristaque hirsutus equina.
870 sic cursum in medios rapidus dedit. aestuat ingens
uno in corde pudor mixtoque insania luctu,
[et furiis agitatus amor, et conscia virtus.]
    atque hic Aenean magna ter voce vocavit.
Aeneas agnovit enim, laetusque precatur:
875 'sic pater ille deum faciat, sic altus Apollo!
incipias conferre manum.'
tantum effatus, et infesta subit obvius hasta.
ille autem: 'quid me erepto, saevissime, nato
terres? haec via sola fuit, qua perdere posses.
880 nec mortem horremus, nec divum parcimus ulli.
desine: nam venio moriturus, et haec tibi porto
dona prius.' dixit, telumque intorsit in hostem;
inde aliud super atque aliud figitque volatque
ingenti gyro; sed sustinet aureus umbo.
885 ter circum adstantem laevos equitavit in orbes,
tela manu iaciens; ter secum Troïus heros
immanem aerato circumfert tegmine silvam.
inde ubi tot traxisse moras, tot spicula taedet
vellere, et urgetur pugna congressus iniqua,
890 multa movens animo iam tandem erumpit, et inter
bellatoris equi cava tempora conicit hastam.
tollit se arrectum quadrupes, et calcibus auras
verberat, effusumque equitem super ipse secutus
implicat, eiectoque incumbit cernuus armo.

895 clamore incendunt caelum Troësque Latinique.
advolat Aeneas vaginaque eripit ensem,
et super haec: 'ubi nunc Mezentius acer, et illa
effera vis animi?' contra Tyrrhenus, ut auras
suspiciens hausit caelum, mentemque recepit:
900 'hostis amare, quid increpitas, mortemque minaris?
nullum in caede nefas; nec sic ad proelia veni;
nec tecum meus haec pepigit mihi foedera Lausus.
unum hoc, per si qua est victis venia hostibus, oro:
corpus humo patiare tegi. scio acerba meorum
905 circumstare odia: hunc, oro, defende furorem;
et me consortem nati concede sepulchro.'
haec loquitur iuguloque haud inscius accipit ensem,
undantique animam diffundit in arma cruore.

Abbreviations

abl.	ablative	lit.	literally
absol.	absolute	m.	masculine
acc.	accusative	n.	neuter
adj.	adjective	neg.	negative
adv.	adverb	nom.	nominative
c.	common	pass.	passive
cf.	compare	perf.	perfect
conj.	conjunction	pl.	plural
dat.	dative	pluperf.	pluperfect
f.	feminine	predic.	predicative
fut.	future	prep.	preposition
gen.	genitive	pres.	present
imperat.	imperative	pron.	pronoun
indecl.	indeclinable	sing.	singular
infin.	infinitive	subj.	subjunctive
interrog.	interrogative	trans.	transitive
intrans.	intransitive	voc.	vocative

Notes

1. **interea**: the poet turns our attention away from the warfare on earth. **panditur**: a majestic word, suggesting the splendours of Olympus. Historic present tenses are common in poetry, see also the verbs in lines 4 and 5.
2. **divum**: gen. pl. for *divorum*.
3f. **terras...Latinos**: neatly combines Jupiter's overall power and his particular immediate concern. **Dardanidum**: gen. pl. for *Dardanidarum*.
5. **considunt tectis**: subject is the gods, 'they sit down in the hall'. **bipatentibus**: i.e. with doors at either end, for east and west. **ipse**: i.e. Jupiter, emphasising his supreme position.
7. **versa**: supply *est*. **vobis versa retro**: 'has been reversed by you'. **vobis**: dat. of the agent. **certatis**: from *certo* 'you strive'.
8. **Italiam**: i.e. 'the peoples of Italy'. **bello**: *in* omitted.
9. **quae**: with *discordia*, supply *est*, 'what is (this) disobedience...?' **quis**: = *qui* (adj.) like *quae* in this line, 'what fear'. **contra vetitum**: 'against what has been forbidden (by me)'. **aut hos aut hos**: the two sides, i.e. the Italians and the Trojans.
10. **arma sequi**: 'to pursue (a policy of) warfare'. **ferrumque lacessere**: 'and provoke a battle'.
11. **ne arcessite**: a poetic construction.
12. **olim**: used here with future meaning.
13. **exitium...apertas**: instead of having *Alpes apertas* as an abl. absol. the poet makes the phrase a second object of the verb, 'will (force) open the Alps and launch great destruction'. References to events in Roman history help to link the poem with the Romans of Virgil's own day. The reference here is to the invasion of Italy by the Carthaginian general Hannibal in 218 B.C.
14. **res rapuisse**: i.e. 'to take plunder'. **licebit**: supply *vobis*.

15. **nunc:** 'for the moment'. **placitum:** 'decided (by me)'.
16. **paucis:** supply *verbis dixit*. **at non:** two monosyllables along with the pointed repitition of *pauca* emphasise Venus' annoyance and her long speech. **contra:** adv. here.
17. Half lines such as this are possibly due to the fact that Virgil did not have time to revise the *Aeneid*.
18. **rerumque:** 'and of the world'.
19. **aliud quid sit:** 'what other (power) is there?'
20. **ut:** 'how', note that the following three verbs are in the subjunctive. Repeat *ut* with *Turnusque*. **feratur:** 'rushes'.
21. **per medios:** the deeds of Turnus *per medios* (of the Trojans) were described in Book IX. **tumidusque secundo Marte:** 'and proud in the success of his warfare'. In these two lines Virgil, through Venus, gives a striking description of the proud, restless and impulsive Turnus.
22. **non clausa...moenia:** 'no longer do the closed fortifications protect...' Note the limping rhythm of this line emphasising Venus' anxiety.
23. **quin:** 'in fact'. **proelia miscent:** 'they engage in battle'.
25. **abest:** Aeneas is away seeking help from Evander, a Greek now settled in Italy. **levari:** infinitive form of impersonal passive, 'there to be a relief'.
26. **iterum:** i.e. as the Greek army had once besieged the walls of the first Troy. Note the emphatic repetition of *iterum* in line 28.
27. **nec non:** = *et*.
28. **Arpis:** Arpi was a city in Apulia; according to the legend followed by Virgil it was being founded at this time by Diomedes, son of Tydeus, one of the Greek commanders in the Trojan War. The Latin request for Diomedes' help is in fact refused in Book XI.
29. **mea vulnera restant:** 'wounds still await me'. Venus had been wounded by Diomedes in the Trojan War.
30. A bitter remark: Venus, a goddess, is keeping the mortals who wish to wound her waiting by being on Olympus.
31. **pace:** 'approval'.
32. **petiere:** shortened form of *petierunt*. **luant...neque iuveris:** 'let them pay for...and do not help'. **iuveris:** a perf. subj. used with *ne* for a negative command; **neque** = *et ne*.

33. **secuti:** supply *sunt*.
34. **superi manesque:** i.e. the Olympian gods and the ghosts of mortals, e.g. Hector (Book II) and Anchises (Book VI). The second part of the sentence is forcefully expressed with two monosyllables and emphasis put on *tua quisquam*.
35. **condere:** supply *quisquam potest...illis*.
36. **quid repetam:** probably subj. 'why should I mention again...?' **exustas...classes:** Iris, sent by Juno, persuaded the Trojan women to set fire to the fleet in a vain attempt to force Aeneas to remain in Sicily. cf. Book V 606ff.
37. **quid:** supply *repetam*. **tempestatum regem:** no sooner had the Trojan fleet set sail from Sicily than Juno went to Aeolus, king of the winds, and prevailed on him to release his storm winds which wrecked the Trojan fleet on the shore of Africa. cf. Book I 50ff.
38. **Aeolia:** expression of place, *ex* omitted. **actam nubibus:** 'sent from the clouds'.
39. **manes:** object of *movet*, here 'fiends' or 'demons'.
40. **sors rerum:** with *haec*, 'this part of creation'. **movet:** 'she stirs up', subject is Juno, implicated in the actions mentioned in lines 36-8 but as yet unnamed. **superis immissa repente:** 'suddenly unleashed upon the upper world'. In Book VII 323ff. Virgil describes the furious activity of Allecto.
41. **Italum:** see note on *divum*, line 2. **bacchata:** see note on *versa*, line 7.
42. **nil...moveor:** 'I am not excited any longer by a (future) empire'. **super:** here followed by the abl. = *de*. **speravimus:** 'I did hope for'. **ista:** refers loosely to *imperio*. Venus is gently reminding Jupiter of his promise in Book I 279.
43. **fortuna fuit:** supply *nobis*. Note the alliteration, a mark of Virgil's style. Note also the repetition of v in the second half of the line.
44f. Note the bitterness of the phrase *quam...dura* with the two monosyllables and the adj. *dura* first word of the line. Venus cannot bring herself to mention Juno by name. **quam det:** note the subj., marking the generic use of *quam* 'the sort which'.
46. **liceat:** supply *mihi*, 'may I be allowed'.
47. **liceat:** 'may it be allowed that my grandson...'
48. **sane...iactetur:** 'by all means let Aeneas be tossed'.

50. **hunc:** = *Ascanium.* **valeam:** '(but) may I be able'. **pugnae:** probably dat. 'from the fight'.

51. Amathus and Paphus were two towns on the south coast of Cyprus. According to one legend Venus came ashore at Paphus after she was born from the sea-foam. Another legend has her landing on Cythera, an island off the south of Greece. Note the scansion of Ămăthūs.

52. **inglorius:** refers to Ascanius. Idalium was a mountain town on Cyprus. All four places were closely connected with the worship of Venus or Aphrodite as the Greeks knew her.

53. **exigat:** 'let him live out'. **hic:** 'in one of these places'. **iubeto:** sing. imperat. of *iubeo.* Here *iubeo* is followed by the subj. construction; **iubeto (ut) Karthago premat:** 'give your order that Carthage should oppress...', see line 12.

54. **inde:** i.e. from Ausonia (Italy). **nihil obstabit:** 'there will be no opposition'.

55f. **Tyriis:** Carthage was a Phoenician colony, by tradition founded from Tyre in 814 B.C. but probably rather later. Rome and Carthage came into conflict and the Punic Wars ended in 146 B.C. with the destruction of Carthage. **quid iuvit:** 'what benefit was it...?' The subject of *evadere* and *fugisse* is Ascanius appearing unnamed in *medium,* 'that he escaped...and fled through the middle of...'. Line 56 refers to the burning of Troy (Book II) and 57 to the years of wandering over the sea (Book III).

57. **exhausta pericula:** with *tot* after *per,* 'and so many dangers he endured'.

59. **non satius:** supply *fuisset,* 'wouldn't it have been better...'

60. **quo:** 'where'.

61. **iterumque revolvere:** i.e. to undergo the fate of Troy all over again. Venus is suggesting that, if the Trojans had known what they were going to face in Italy, they would not have decided to leave Troy.

62. **da:** 'grant' or 'allow', + dat. Supply *dixit* as verb to *Iuno.*

63. **silentia:** Juno may have been silent about her feelings towards the Trojans, but she had been at work behind the scenes, e.g. Bk. I 34ff., Book II 612ff., Bk. V 604ff., Bk. VII 323ff., Bk. IX 1ff. Virgil contrasts her outward aloofness – *regia...alta...obductum* with her inner passion – *furore gravi.*

64. **verbis vulgare**: see note on line 43.

65. **Aenean**: the so-called Greek acc. form of Aeneas. **hominum quisquam divumque**: a scornful phrase, 'Did anyone, human or divine...' **quisquam**: recalls Venus' question in line 34.

66. **hostem se inferre**: 'inflict himself as an enemy on'.

67. **fatis auctoribus**: an abl. absol. like *Caesare duce*, 'at the instigation of the fates'. **esto**: 'I grant you', lit. 'let it be', the imperat. of *sum*.

68. Supply 'but' before *Cassandrae*. Juno agrees that the fates did authorise Aeneas' journey but attempts to minimise the importance of his destiny by linking it to the ravings of a half-mad priestess. **furiis**: abstract nouns in Latin usually have concrete meanings when plural, e.g. *amor* – love, *amores* – love affairs, here *furiis* – 'mad ravings'.

69. **hortati sumus**: 'did I encourage him'. Juno is referring to Aeneas' recent journey to seek help from Evander.

70. Supply *hortati sumus*. *Hortor* is rarely used with the infin. construction. **summam belli**: 'the chief responsibility in the war'. **puero**: 'to a (mere) boy'. **credere**: goes with both parts of the line.

71. Supply *hortati sumus* again, *agitare* goes with both parts of the line. Juno is referring to the request for help that Aeneas is making to the Etruscans at Evander's suggestion. cf. Bk. VIII 470-519, Bk. X 146-56. **fidem**: 'loyalty'.

72. **nostra**: 'mine', cf. *hortati sumus* in line 69. **fraudem**: here 'harm'.

73. **hic**: i.e. in this action. **demissa...Iris**: a reply to Venus in line 38.

74. **indignum est**: Juno is being very sarcastic and deliberately picks up a point made by Venus, see line 27, 'it is unfair, (so you say)...' Note the pointed use of *patria*, contrasted with *aliena* in line 78.

75. **nascentem**: Aeneas is attempting to establish a second Troy in Italy. **consistere**: 'take a firm stand'. **patria**: here an adj.

76. Juno is suggesting that Turnus has a more divine ancestry than Aeneas. Supply *erat* to both parts of the line.

77. **quid** + acc. and infin.: 'what about the fact that the Trojans...'

78. **arva aliena**: 'farmlands that belong to others'. **iugo**: possibly a pun; either literally the yoke of ploughing oxen or the yoke of captivity and slavery.

79. Supply *Troianos* or *eos* as subject of *legere* and *abducere*. **quid... legere**: lit. 'what about them picking their fathers-in-law'. **gremiis**:

'from their loved ones'. **pactas**: supply *puellas* or *virgines*. The plurals are an exaggeration as Aeneas is the only one to try and gain a Latin bride by his wooing of Lavinia who was betrothed to Turnus. It was normal for the fathers-in-law to do the choosing; Juno is portraying the Trojans as uncivilised brigands.

80. **manu**: 'with (outstretched) hand'. Supply 'but' before *praefigere*.

81f. **Aenean**: see note to line 65. **Graium**: see note on *divum*, line 2. Juno is referring to an incident described in the *Iliad* (V 315f) where Aphrodite rescued Aeneas from Diomedes. It was Apollo who covered Aeneas in a cloud when Aphrodite herself was wounded (V 344f). Strict accuracy did not concern Juno.

82. **viro**: sarcastic use of the meaning 'hero' for *vir*.

83. It was Cybele who turned the ships into nymphs, cf. Bk. IX 107ff. Once again Juno is not concerned with accuracy.

84. **aliquid...contra iuvisse**: 'to help...a little in reply'. *Aliquid* and *contra* are both adverbial. Note the emphatic *nos* to answer *tu*, line 81. **nos**: 'I', see notes to lines 69 and 72.

85. Juno picks up Venus' words (line 25) and turns them into a wish that Aeneas and Venus should stay in one of Venus' homes, cf. Venus' words in line 51f.

87. **gravidam bellis**: 'bursting for war'. The metaphor is of a pregnant animal. **temptas**: here has the sense of 'interfere' or 'meddle with'.

88. **nos**: see note to line 84. **tibi**: 'on you', i.e. against you. **fundo**: here = *funditus* 'completely'.

89. **an...qui**: 'or wasn't it that one who....'. The reference to Paris is clarified by *Dardanius adulter* (92). **miseros**: a sarcastic echo of line 61. Note scansion Trōăs. Paris was asked to decide which of three goddesses, Juno, Venus and Athena was the most beautiful. He chose Venus because she offered him the most beautiful woman in the world, Helen queen of Sparta, as his wife. This judgement accounts for Juno's implacable hatred of the Trojans and her opposition to Venus. Athena also supported the Greeks in the Trojan war.

90. **quae causa fuit**: 'what was the reason that', here the infin. construction follows instead of the more normal gerund.

92. **me duce**: abl. absol. Note the emphatic beginning to this line and the next one.

94. **tum**: emphatic, 'that was the time when you should have feared for your people'. Supply *te* to *decuit*, *tuis* is dat. after *metuisse*.

95. Juno ends her speech with a forceful alliteration.

97. **vario**: 'with divided assent', i.e. some agreed with one speaker, some with another. **ceu**: a simile enables the poet to introduce a contrasting scene and give his poetry variety.

98. **deprensa silvis**: 'caught by the woods'. **caeca**: 'unseen', 'invisible'. Note how the repetition of the verb *fremunt* links the simile to the event.

99. **prodentia**: 'giving warning of'.

100. **rerum**: 'over the world'. cf. note to line 18.

101. **infit**: in emphatic position. **deum**: gen. pl. Note the strong alliteration.

102. **solo**: 'from its foundations', cf. note on *fundo*, line 88.

103. **posuere**: for *posuerunt*. The word has an intransitive sense here, i.e. 'they abated'. **placida**: in a proleptic sense, 'the sea subdued its surface to a calm.' Note the alliteration.

105. **Ausonios coniungi...haud licitum**: supply *est*, 'it is not permitted that Italians should be joined...'

107. **quae...hodie**: 'whatever fortune each has today'. **quam...secat spem**: 'whatever hope each pursues', *seco spem* perhaps like *seco viam* 'I make my way'.

108. **fuat**: 'whether he be...or...', lit. 'let him be'. *Fuat* is an old form of the pres. subj. of *sum*; archaic language is appropriate to the lofty dignity of Jupiter. **nullo discrimine habebo**: 'I will make no distinction', take this before *Tros Rutulusne fuat*.

109. **fatis Italum**: see note to line 41, 'through the (good) fortune of the Itali'.

110. **Troiae**: for *Troianorum*.

111. **sua...ferent**: 'the undertaking of each will bring him toil or good fortune'. Subject of *ferent* is *exorsa sua*.

112. **rex...idem**: supply *est*.

113. The most binding oath for a god was one by the river Styx. Here the oath is combined with Jupiter's ratifying nod. The lines *Stygii... Olympum* are repeated from Bk. IX 104-6. **fratris**: i.e. Pluto, king of the underworld, who was Jupiter's brother.

116. **finis fandi**: see note to line 43. **aureo** scanned *aurēo*.

117. This section ends with a solemn procession such as many Romans would have seen involving consuls. **quem**: i.e. Jupiter. **caelicolae medium quem ducunt**: 'whom the gods surrounded (*medium*) and escorted'.
118. This is the stage events on earth had reached at the end of Bk. IX. **circum**: adverbial. **portis...viros**: 'at all the gates they press to lay the men low with slaughter'. The use of the infin. after *instant* relies on the sense of 'desire to'.
120. **vallis**: 'inside the palisade', lit. 'by the ramparts'.
121. Supply *est* with *spes*. **miseri**: cf. lines 61 and 89.
122. **rara...corona**: 'with a widely-spaced circle'. **nequiquam et rara**: very emphatic – their high towers give none of the expected advantages and their defenders are inadequate. **cinxere**: for *cinxerunt*.
123. Virgil is using names found in Homer's *Iliad*.
124. **Assaraci**: these are named after Assaracus, the legendary king of Troy and grandfather of Aeneas. **senior**: 'an old man', describing Thymbris.
125. **ambo**: 'two'. In the *Iliad* Sarpedon was a staunch ally of the Trojans.
126. **alta**: 'mountainous' or 'noble'.
127. Subject of *fert* is *Lymesius Acmon*. **conixus**: from *conitor*, 'straining'. The position of the *ingens saxum* straddling *toto...corpore* cleverly reinforces the description of the rock's overwhelming size. Its vast weight finds an echo in the heavy spondees.
129. **minor**: this either refers to his stature or to his strength and courage. **Menestheo**: scanned *Mĕnēsthēō* by synizesis, cf. *aureō*, line 116. This man should not be confused with Mnestheus, line 143. Clytius was killed by Turnus in Bk. IX.
130. **hi iaculis**: supply *certant*.
131. **moliri**: 'to hurl'.
132. **iustissima cura**: 'the very rightful concern'. Venus was concerned (a) because Ascanius was her grandson and (b) because he had an important role in the future Roman race.
133. **Dardanius**: to be taken with *puer*. **caput honestum**: acc. retained in the passive, defining the extent of *detectus*, 'his lovely head

uncovered'; *honestum* is a poetical word for *pulchrum*. Ascanius had been told by Apollo (Bk. IX 656) to take no further part in the fighting.

134. **quae dividit:** 'which is set in'.

135. Supply *est* to *decus*, 'is an ornament'. **vel quale ebur:** 'or like ivory which'.

136. **inclusum buxo:** 'inlaid in boxwood'. **būxō aūt:** hiatus after -o is quite common in Virgil. The terebinth tree, pistacia terebinthus, produces a black wood which would make a striking contrast to ivory.

137. **cui:** 'for whom', i.e. 'his'. **fusos...accipit:** 'his white neck was covered with flowing hair'.

138. The object of *subnectit* is *crines* above.

139. The technique of having a character addressed directly by the author (here Ismarus) is called 'apostrophe'.

140. **vulnera...veneno:** 'aiming your blows and priming your arrows with poison'.

141. **Maeonia...domo:** abl. 'from a Lydian house'. **generose:** voc. **pinguia culta:** 'rich arable land'. **dōmō ŭbĭ:** see note to *buxo aut*, line 136.

142. **Pactolus:** Midas, king of Phrygia, had been granted by Bacchus the privilege that everything he touched turned to gold. When this extended to his food and his life was in danger, he was told to wash in the river Pactolus. Ever after the sands of this river were mixed with gold-dust.

143f. In Bk. IX 779f. Mnestheus rallies the beleaguered Trojans to drive Turnus back when he was causing havoc inside the Trojan camp. **pristina:** 'of yesterday', agrees with *gloria* but refers to *Turni pulsi*. **aggere murorum:** 'from the rampart of the walls', with *pulsi*.

145. **hinc:** 'from him'. Virgil linked various allies of Aeneas with places in Italy and Rome; in this case he is referring to Capua in Campania.

146. **illi:** i.e. the Rutulians and the Trojans. **inter sese certamina contulerant:** 'had engaged in the struggles with each other'. **sese:** = *se*. The tense of *contulerant* indicates that the reader's attention is about to be switched to another subject. **duri:** to be taken more probably with *belli*.

147. Bk. VIII decribed Aeneas' journey to Evander's humble city to seek his help in the war; at line 607 the narrative left him on his return journey meeting up with Tarchon, the leader of the Etruscans. Since then the poet has been describing the attacks on the Trojan camp in Aeneas' absence.

148. **ab Euandro**: 'after leaving Evander'. **ingressus**: supply *est*, *ingredior* here with the dat., more usually with acc. or *in* + acc. **castris Etruscis**: Tarchon's camp. Evander had migrated from Greece to Italy and established a small city on the Palatine hill – later to become one of the seven hills of Rome.

149. **genus**: 'high birth', 'noble lineage'.

150ff. **-ve...-ve**: here for *-que...-que*. **Mezentius...edocet**: an easier word order is *edocet quae arma Mezentius sibi conciliet, violentaque pectora Turni*. **quae arma**: 'what forces'. **violenta pectora**: 'the violent temper', *violentus* and *violentia*, both very strong words, are only used for Turnus in the *Aeneid*. Mezentius, once a ruthless tyrant, had been driven out by his people and had taken refuge with Turnus.

152. **humanis rebus**: 'in human resources'. **quae fiducia**: 'what (little) reliance'.

154. **libera fati**: 'freed from its fate', *liber* is more commonly with abl., here with gen.

155f. The Lydian people, i.e. the Etruscans, were fated only to suceed if they entrusted themselves to a foreign leader – *externo commissa duci*. The Etruscans were believed to have migrated to Italy from western Asia Minor.

156. **dŭci Aēnēĭā**: note the hiatus.

157. **prima tenet**: 'took the lead'. We must presume that this ship was one of the original ones which sailed from Troy. **rostro...leones**: 'with Phrygian lions fixed to its prow', for the case of *leones* see the note on *caput*, line 133. Lions were sacred to Cybele who allowed Aeneas to build his fleet from her sacred pines growing on Mt. Ida.

158. **super**: adv. i.e. the upper part of the prow. **Ida**: here a figurehead representing the mountain near Troy.

160. **Pallasque**: this is the first mention of the young man who plays a big role in this book. He had been sent by his father Evander to help the Trojans and was entrusted to Aeneas' care; here he sits close to Aeneas but there is a hint of doom to come in the phrase *Pallasque sinistro*.

161. **adfixus**: 'sitting close'. **sidera...iter**: *iter* is in apposition to *sidera*, 'the stars (guiding) their journey through the dark night'.

162. **passus**: for *passus sit* from *patior*, 'I suffer', the subject is Aeneas. Pallas was questioning Aeneas about his travels.

163. This line constitutes a second beginning to Book X. **pandite**: cf. *panditur*, line 1. **Helicona**: Greek acc. Mt. Helicon in Boeotia in Greece was considered to be the home of the Muses. Virgil used this line previously (Bk. VII 641) when introducing the catalogue of Turnus' forces. Such catalogues are a regular feature of epic poetry, beginning with the *Iliad* where Book II is largely taken up by a catalogue of the Greek and Trojan forces. Even Milton felt obliged to continue this traditional feature – *Paradise Lost* Bk. I 376ff. A catalogue is by its nature rather repetitive but Virgil maintains the interest of his audience by a variety of devices.

164. **quae manus**: 'what band'. This indirect question depends on *cantus*, i.e. 'the song (relating) what band'.

165. **pelago**: 'over the sea'. **Aenean**: see note to line 65.

166. **Massicus**: Virgil may have taken this name from Mt. Massicus in Campania. **Tigri**: the name of the ship; it presumably had a tigress as its figurehead. **aerata**: describing *Tigri* not *aequora*.

167. **iuvenum**: often used to denote men of military age.

168. **liquere**: for *liquerunt*. **quis**: for *quibus*. **tela**: supply *sunt*, 'whose weapons are...'.

169. **umeris**: abl. 'on their shoulders'.

170. **una**: 'along with (them) was'.

171. **aurato...puppis**: 'his ship shone with the gilded (figurehead of) Apollo'.

172. **mater**: 'his mother-city'.

173. **belli**: 'in war'. **ast**: = *at*. **Ilva**: supply *dederat*.

175. **ille**: 'that (well-known)'. **divumque**: see note to line 2.

176. **parent**: some editors suggest this word = *apparent* 'are clear'; it is more likely being used in the sense of 'obey', 'submit to', i.e. 'reveal their secrets to'.

177. **linguae volucrum**: 'cries of birds'.

178. **mille rapit**: 'he hurries along a thousand men'.
179. **hos...solo**: 'Pisae, an Etruscan city in its situation (*solo*), but Alphean in origin, orders these to obey him'. Virgil connects Pisae with Pisa in S.W. Greece near the river Alpheus, but there is no evidence for this.
182. **adiciunt**: 'they add'. The subject for this verb is the four groups mentioned in the next two lines.
183. **domo**: abl. of origin, 'from their homes at Caere'. Caere was one of the wealthiest of the Etruscan towns.
184. **Graviscae**: Cato remarked on the *gravem aerem* of this place; this phrase must lie behind Virgil's description here.
185. **Ligurum**: Ligurian tribes occupied coastal areas from the Rhone to the northern boundary of Etruria.
186. **transierim**: perf. subj. for a polite assertion, 'I would not pass you by'. **Cinyre**: the spelling is uncertain, see also note on *Ismare*, line 139. **paucis**: for *a paucis*. **Cupavo**: another voc. agreeing with *comitate*. **comitate**: from *comito*, 'accompanied by few'.
188ff. The reference here is to Cycnus, father of Cupavo, who was enamoured of Phaethon. When the latter was burnt up in the runaway chariot of the sun, Cycnus was broken-hearted and was turned into a swan. **vestrum**: i.e. yours and your mother's. **insigne**: in apposition to *pinnae*, 'and are the badge of...'.
190. **sororum**: Phaethon's sisters were turned into poplars.
191. **musa**: abl. 'with a song'. Note the repetition of 'm'.
192. **canentem...senectam**: 'as he sang he brought on himself a (white) old age with soft plumage'.
193. **voce**: i.e. 'as he sang'.
194. **filius**: 'his son' i.e. Cupavo. **comitatus**: 'accompanying' from *comitor*. Note the alliteration.
195. **Centaurum**: the name of Cupavo's ship. **ille**: the figurehead of the ship, presumably in the form of a centaur.
196. **instat**: takes the dat. The figurehead was evidently poised on its hind legs (*arduus*) about to hurl a large rock.
197. Scansion will help translation of this line; the subject is now the ship rather than the figurehead.
198. **ille**: deictic use, 'over there', with *Ocnus*.
199. **Mantus**: a Greek gen. 'of Manto'. The Tuscan river was the Tiber.

200. Virgil was born near Mantua.

201. **dives avis**: 'wealthy in its ancestry', *avis* from *avus* 'ancestor'. **sed...unum**: supply *est*.

202f. **illi**: dat. sing. refers to the city, i.e. 'it has'. **ipsa**: i.e. *Mantua ipsa*, supply *est*. **Tusco...vires**: a sharp contrast with 'but' omitted. These lines are a little obscure. Virgil says that the city is made up of three races each with four peoples and that, while Mantua was their acknowledged capital, the real strength came from the Etruscans. The three races are presumably the Etruscans, the Greeks and Italic people, perhaps the Veneti.

204. **in se**: 'against himself'. **armat**: i.e. 'he forced to take up arms'.

205. **patre Benaco**: 'from his father Benacus'. The river Mincius flowed from lake Benacus, so the god of the river is described as *velatus harundine glauca*. The Mincius does not in fact flow into the sea (*in aequora*) but is a tributary of the Padus, the modern Po.

206. **infesta pinu**: i.e. 'in warships'. Pines provided the bulk of the timber for ships.

207. **gravis**: 'mighty'. **centena arbore**: 'with his hundred tree trunk (oars)'.

208. **spumant...verso**: 'the water foamed as the sea was churned up'.

209. **Triton**: the name and figurehead of Aulestes' ship. **caerula**: with *freta* below, not *concha*.

210f. **cui...praefert**: 'as it sailed along (*cui nanti*) its hairy figurehead (*hispida frons*) portrayed a man down to its flanks'. **in...alvus**: a sharp contrast, supply 'but'; see note to line 203.

212. Note the alliteration of 's' for the foaming water.

213. **ter denis**: large numbers rarely appear in Latin poetry in their simplest form.

214. **subsidio Troiae**: predic. dat. 'as a help for Troy'. **aere**: the oars were probably tipped with bronze.

215. **caelo**: preposition 'from' has been omitted.

216. **Olympum**: 'the sky'.

218. **velis**: from *velum* 'sail' not *volo*.

219. **atque**: exclamatory, 'and suddenly'. **medio in spatio**: 'in the middle of his course'. **chorus suarum comitum**: 'a band of his own companions', a reference to the incident in Bk. IX 77f. where the goddess Cybele (here called Cybebe) turned Aeneas' ships into sea-nymphs to prevent them being destroyed by fire.

220-3 Best divided into 2 or 3 sentences in English.

221. **numen maris:** 'power over the sea'.

222. **pariter:** adv. 'beside him'.

224. **lustrantque choreis:** i.e. 'and they danced around him'.

225. **quae doctissima:** supply *erat*, 'the one of them who was most skilled'. **fandi:** gen. of gerund of *for*, 'in speech'.

226. **ipsaque...eminet:** 'emerged in person to her waist', *dorso* lit. 'with her back'.

227. **laeva:** abl. 'with her left hand'. **tacitis undis:** 'in the calm water'.

228. **ignarum:** supply *eum* i.e. Aeneas. **deum:** gen. pl. see note on *divum* line 2. **gens:** voc., 'descendant'.

229. **velis:** dat. 'for the sails'.

230. **pinus:** pl. 'pines'.

231f. **nunc:** supply 'but' to mark the contrast. **perfidus Rutulus:** i.e. Turnus. **praecipites nos premebat:** 'was driving us headlong'. **flamma:** abl. with *ferro*.

234. **genetrix:** i.e. Cybele, 'our mother'. **miserata:** from *miseror*, 'in pity'. **hanc faciem refecit:** 'remade us in this form'.

235. **dedit:** 'granted that we'.

237. **horrentes Marte:** 'bristling with war'.

238f. **Arcas eques:** a sing. collective, 'Arcadian cavalry'. **loca...tenet:** 'occupy their appointed positions'. This group, we must assume, had been sent by Evander overland and had joined up with some of Tarchon's forces to meet Aeneas at an agreed place.

239. **medias...turmas:** 'to station squadrons of horsemen in between to oppose them'. This phrase explains 'Turnus' decision' (*sententia Turno*), line 240.

240. **castris:** i.e. the Trojans' camp.

241. **Aurora veniente:** 'as dawn is breaking'. **vocari in arma:** 'be called to arms'.

242. **primus:** 'as your first priority', 'immediately'.

243. **invictum:** with *clipeum* above; note its emphatic position stressing the invincibility of the shield. In Bk. VIII 369ff. Venus persuades Vulcan to make a divine suit of armour for Aeneas. **ignipotens:** i.e. Vulcan.

244. **putaris:** shortened form of fut. perf. *putaveris*.

246. **dextra:** abl. 'with her right hand'. **altam:** with *puppim* below.

247. **haud ignara modi:** 'well aware of the method'. A reference, perhaps humorous, to the nymph's previous experience as a ship herself. **illa:** i.e. the nymph.

248. **et...et:** 'than either...or'. **iaculo, sagitta:** abl. of comparison. **ventis aequante:** 'equalling the winds (in speed)'.

249. **aliae:** supply *naves*. **inscius:** i.e. not knowing why the ship had increased its speed.

250. **animos omine tollit:** 'he raised his spirits as a result of the omen'.

251. **brevitur:** with *precatur*.

252. **parens deum:** 'mother of the gods', i.e. Cybele. **cordi:** predicative dat. **cui...cordi:** 'to whom Dindyma is a delight', 'who delights in Dindyma'.

253. **ad frena:** 'harnessed'. Cybele was usually portrayed with lions.

254. **propinques:** transitive here with *augurium*, 'may you hasten on your prophecy'.

255. **pede secundo:** singular for plural.

256. **effatus:** supply *est*. **revoluta...dies:** note *dies* is f. here; 'the returning (*revoluta*) day was now hurrying with its full light'. Note the repeated 'r'.

257. **fugarat:** shortened form of *fugaverat*.

258. **principio:** adv. 'to begin with'. **edicit sequantur:** 'he gave an order that they should follow'; *ut* has been omitted after *edicit*.

259. **animos...armis:** 'tune their spirits for battle'. Note again the alliterations and that the line ends abruptly in a monosyllable, a comparatively rare ending, cf. lines 2, 107, 228.

260. Subject is Aeneas.

261. **cum deinde:** emphatic, 'when immediately'.

261f. Note the clever order of the poetry. The shield is lifted, catches the sun and there is the immediate shout of recognition and welcome from the Trojans.

263. **spes...iras:** '(this) renewed hope roused their fury'.

265. The simile of flying cranes was borrowed from the opening lines of *Iliad* Bk. III. **dant signa atque aethera tranant:** 'call out and fly across the sky'.

266. **clamore secundo:** 'with exultant cries'.

267. **Rutulo regi:** i.e. Turnus. **videri:** an historic infin. to convey drama, tension and suddenness, translate as a perf. tense, 'they seemed'. **ea:** i.e. the shouting and the renewed fury, see lines 262f.

269. **totumque...aequor:** 'the whole sea gliding in with ships'. The Rutulians no longer see just waves rolling in, but ships.

270. **apex:** 'his helmet'. **capiti:** 'on his head', i.e. on Aeneas' head. **cristis a vertice:** 'from the plumes from its peak'.

272. **non secus ac:** 'just as'. **liquida nocte:** an expression of time. **si quando:** 'sometimes'. **cometae:** note *cometes* is a masc. word; this is perhaps a veiled reference to the comet seen after Julius Caesar's death.

273. **lugubre:** adv. 'with foreboding'. Sirius, the dog-star, for a country dweller marked the period of greatest heat during the summer.

275. **nascitur:** 'rises'. **laevo:** 'ill-omened'. **contristat lumine:** a striking phrase that seems almost contradictory. Virgil is describing sultry weather when the sky lacks brightness.

276. **haud:** to be taken with *cessit*.

277. *praecipere* and *pellere* follow *fiducia* with the sense of 'a confident desire to'. **praecipere:** i.e. to get to the shore before the enemy ships could. **pellere terra:** 'repulse from the land'.

278. This line is missing from two of the main manuscripts and should probably be omitted here; it is a repeat of Bk. IX 127.

279. **optastis:** shortened form of *optavistis*. **quod:** = *id quod*. **quod optastis:** 'what you have wished for'. **perfringere dextra:** explains *quod*, 'to crush them by force', i.e. 'with your swords'.

280. **in manibus...viri:** supply *est*, 'war itself is now in your grasp, men'; i.e. real war as distinguished from besieging the camp. **esto:** 3rd sing. imperat. of *sum*. **nunc esto quisque:** 'now let each of you be'.

281. **referto:** cf. on *esto* above, 'let (each) recall'.

282. **patrum laudes:** 'things that brought praise to your fathers'. **ultro:** 'of one's own accord', here 'let's take the initiative and...'

283. **dum trepidi:** supply *sunt*. **egressisque...prima:** supply *eis*, lit. 'and to them having disembarked their first steps totter'.

284. This proverbial remark appears in other Roman writers; Ovid, for example, has *audentes deus ipse iuvat* in Met. X. 586. In modern times it has become a proverb and a motto. It is a fitting climax to Turnus' rousing speech.

285f. **quos...muros:** *possit* goes with both infins., 'whom he could lead against (the enemy) and to whom he could entrust the besieged walls'. With Aeneas' return by sea, Turnus now has to divide his forces into two groups.

288f. **pontibus**: 'by gangways'. **servare** and **credere**: historic infins., see note on *videri* line 267. **servare recursus**: *recursus* is acc. pl., 'they watched for the ebbing'. **brevibus se credere**: 'they entrusted themselves to the shallows', *brevibus* is a n. pl. noun here.

290. **per remos**: a vague phrase, probably 'by rowing'. **alii**: supply a verb, perhaps 'came to land'.

291. The main verb is *advertit* line 293. **qua...spirant**: 'where the shallows did not surge'. **remurmurat**: Virgil is describing the noise (*murmur*) made by the water as it breaks on the shore and retreats (*re-*).

292. After *sed* supply *qua* from above. **mare...aestu**: 'the sea glided in with a surging swell unobstructed'.

296. **sulcumque...premat**: 'let it cut its own furrow'.

297. **tali statione**: 'on such a beach'.

298. **arrepta...semel**: 'once land has been seized', 'once we have secured a landing'.

299f. **effatus**: supply *est*. **consurgere** and **inferre**: historic infins., 'they rose to the oars (*tonsis*) and drove'.

301. **tenent siccum**: 'hold firmly the dry land'. **sedere**: for *sederunt* 'they settled'.

302. Another example of apostrophe, cf. line 39, often used by the poet to address a doomed or unfortunate character.

303f. **dorso...diu**: 'while she hung there wavering for a long time supported by the rough spine of rock'.

305. Note the dramatic position of the single word *solvitur* for the sudden break-up of the ship. **viros**: 'her crew'. **exponit**: the correct technical term for disembarkation, cf. line 288, here used for the unceremonious dumping of the crew into the sea.

306. **quos**: i.e. Tarchon's crew, to be taken before *fragmina*.

307. **unda relabens**: 'the undertow'.

308f. The rhythm of these two lines mirrors the meaning. **rapit**: 'he hurries along'. **contra**: adv. 'to oppose them'.

310. **signa canunt**: 'the signals (for battle) blare out'.

311. **omen pugnae**: i.e. Aeneas' initial success is prophetic of the final outcome.

312ff. Theron and the other Latins killed by Aeneas up to line 344 play no other part in the *Aeneid*. There are a number of similar incidents in Homer's *Iliad* when the hero kills several of the enemy, each named individually, sometimes with other family or personal information briefly added. **virum maximus**: 'tallest of men', cf. note on *divum* line 2. **ultro**: cf. note to line 282.

313f. **huic**: i.e. Theron. **perque...per**: 'through both...and'; the repeated *per* replaces *-que*; 'through both his (*huic*) bronze coat of mail and his tunic stiff with gold he (Aeneas) opened his side with his sword (*gladio latus apertum*) and drained it (of blood)'.

315. **ferit**: from *ferio* 'I strike'. **exsectum...perempta**: i.e. his mother died giving him birth.

316. **sacrum**: infants who survived a dangerous birth which killed their mother were consecrated to Apollo, god of medicine and healing. **casus ferri**: 'the hazards of the knife'; the knife that cut him from his mother.

317. **quod licuit parvo**: 'because, when he was young, he was allowed'. **longe**: adv. of space not time. **Cissea**: Greek acc. of Cisseus, cf. *Helicona* line 163.

318. **agmina**: acc. pl. **clava**: abl. sing. **Gyan**: Greek acc. of Gyas.

319. **leto**: = *in letum*. **Herculis arma**: referring to *clava* which was the traditional weapon used by Hercules.

320. **iuvere**: for *iuverunt*. **genitorque Melampus**: 'or (the fact that) Melampus was their father'.

321. **Alcidae**: 'of Alcides'. Hercules as grandson of Alceus was called Alcides. The idea that the earth provided Hercules with labours is a reference to the great distances Hercules travelled when performing them. **usque...dum**: 'as long as'.

322. **voces inertes**: 'idle threats'.

323. **Pharo intorquens...ore**: 'hurling a javelin at Pharus, he planted it in his mouth as he shouted'. An appropriate end for a loud-mouthed person.

324. **tu**: i.e. Cydon line 325. **malas**: acc. of respect with *flaventem*, 'becoming golden on his cheeks'.

325. **nova gaudia**: 'your latest delight', referring to Clytius.

326f. **stratus**: 'felled', from *sterno*. **securus...erant**: 'untroubled by love for young men which you always had'. **iaceres**: 'you would have lain there'.

328. **ni...obvia:** 'if the massed band of your brothers had not been in the way'. **foret:** alternative subj. of *sum*, = *esset*.

329. **septena:** the distributive form, here used for the cardinal form *septem*; cf. *denis* line 213 and *centena* line 207.

330. **partim resultant:** 'some rebounded'.

331. **inrita and stringentia:** both describe *tela*.

332. **alma Venus:** note its position; it is held back to give it more impact. **Achaten:** Greek acc. of Achates, cf. *Aenean* line 65.

333f. **non ullum...quae:** 'not one will my right hand hurl (*dextera torserit*) in vain at the Rutuli, weapons which (*quae*) stuck fast (*steterunt*)...'. **torserit:** a fut. perf.; Aeneas is envisaging a future action from a position even further in the future. **Graium:** gen pl.

335. **Iliacis campis:** preposition omitted, 'on the plains of Troy'.

336. Note how the rhythm of *et iacit* emphasises the launching of the spear.

337. **thoraca:** Greek acc.

338. **ruentem:** 'as he (Maeon) collapsed'.

339f. **dextra:** abl. sing. **traiecto...tenorem:** 'a spear hurled (*hasta missa*) sliced through his (i.e. Alcanor's) arm (*traiecto lacerto*) and sped on at once (*protinus fugit*) holding to its course (*servat tenorem*) and stained with blood'. The unnamed thrower of the spear is Aeneas.

341. **nervis...pependit:** 'hung by its sinews lifeless'.

343f. **contra:** 'in return', 'in retaliation'. **non est licitum:** 'he was not allowed'; supply *ei*. Numitor's throw, though aimed at Aeneas in retaliation for his brother's death, missed its target and merely grazed Achates.

345. **hic:** expression of time not place. This section (345-356) describes the killing done by Aeneas' enemies. Clausus, Halaesus and Messapus all appear in the catalogue of Turnus' forces in Bk. VII. **Curibus:** 'from Cures'. **fidens:** + abl. not the more usual dat. **primaevo corpore:** 'his youthful physique'.

346. **advenit:** 'arrived on the scene'. **ferit:** from *ferio* 'I strike', not *fero*.

347f. **graviter pressa:** 'driven with force'. **pariter...gutture:** 'and by slicing through his windpipe (*traiecto gutture*) as he spoke (*loquentis*) he robbed him of his power of speech and his life at the same time'. This is a bold use of zeugma. **ille:** i.e. Dryops.

350. The subject is still Clausus introduced at line 345. The Thracians were allies of the Trojans in the Trojan War. **Boreae...suprema:** 'from the loftiest race of Boreas'.

353. **manus:** nom. sing., 'a force', 'a band'.

354. **insignis:** with *Messapus* not *equis*, though doubtless it was his horses that made him *insignis* as Neptune's horses were the envy of all. **expellere:** an obj. needs to be supplied. They are trying to drive off the forces of Aeneas and Tarchon as they land.

355. **certatur:** impersonal pass., 'the battle raged'. **limine...Ausoniae:** the poet emphasises the importance of this battle.

356. *ceu* which introduces this simile has been postponed into the next line, 'as when...'. **magno aethere:** 'over the whole sky', preposition omitted.

357. **animis...aequis:** 'with matched courage/blasts and strength'; *animis* is a possible pun, either from *anima* (blasts) or *animus* *(courage)*.

358. Supply *cedunt* from *cedit* to *ipsi* and *nubila*.

359. This line is the main point of the simile, with emphasis put on *anceps*. Note how the rhythm of the second half of the line reflects the stalemate.

361. **haeret...vir:** 'they are locked together foot to foot and closely packed man to man'. Note the striking word order in 360- 1, *acies aciesque...pede pes...viro vir.*

362f. **qua...ripis:** 'where (*qua*) a torrent had spread rolling boulders far and wide and bushes torn from its banks'. **ripis:** abl. of separation. This is a description of a dried-up river bed.

364. Take *ut vidit Pallas* from line 365 before *Arcadas*. **Arcadas... pedestres:** 'the Arcadians unused to advance in infantry formations'. *inferre* is used transitively here as in other authors: e.g. *pedem inferre, signa inferre.*

365. **Latio sequaci:** 'to the pursuing Latins'. *Latium* here stands for *Latini.*

366. **quis:** = *quibus.* **quando:** probably = *quandoquidem* 'since': 'since the rough condition of the terrain (*aspera natura loci*) prompted them (*quis suasit*) to dispense with their horses'.

367. **unum quod:** 'the only thing that...'. **rebus egenis:** 'in the desperate situation'.

371. **patriae aemula laudi:** 'rivalling the fame of my father'. *patriae* from *patrius*.

372. **ne fidete:** a poetic construction for *nolite fidere*. **pedibus:** i.e. escape on foot. Note the emphatic and contrasting positions of *pedibus* and *ferro*.

373. **qua:** 'where', answered by *hac* in next line. **virum:** = *virorum*.

374. **Pallanta:** Greek acc. of Pallas. **patria alta:** 'your noble land'. **reposcit:** 'requires...to be'.

375f. Note the emphatic repetition of *mortali...mortales*. **totidem nobis:** supply *sunt*, 'we have just as many'.

377. **maris magna obice pontus:** *obice* from *obex*, to be taken with *maris*, 'the ocean with a great barrier of sea'.

378. **deest:** supply *nobis*. **pelagus...petemus:** 'will we make for the sea or the Trojan camp?' **pelagus:** a neuter noun is acc. here. Note the scansion *dēest*.

380. **huic:** i.e. Pallas.

381. Lagus and the other six opponents of Pallas are otherwise unknown; notice how Virgil describes Lagus in foreboding terms even before he is named.

382f. **discrimina...dabat:** 'through his middle where (*per medium qua*) his spine divided his ribs'. **discrimina dare:** 'to separate' with dat. **receptat:** a frequentative form of *recipio*, 'he tugs repeatedly at'.

384. **quem:** i.e. Pallas. **super:** adv. 'bending over him'.

385. **sperans:** 'though hoping for...'. **ante:** adv. going with *excipit*.

386. **dum furit crudeli morte sodalis:** 'while in a fury at the cruel death of his comrade'. **incautum:** goes with *ruentem*.

388. **hinc:** used of time rather than place, 'after this'.

389. **ausum:** deponent past participle of audeo, 'having dared'.

390. **cecidistis:** from *cado*.

391. **Daucia proles:** voc. continuing the apostrophe, 'offspring of Daucus'. **Laride:** Greek voc. of Larides.

392. **indiscreta...error:** 'indistinguishable to their parents and a pleasing source of error'. Note that the sentence has changed from a second person subject (*vos*) to a third person one (*suis*).

393. A powerful line with hard-hitting alliteration; *discrimina* is in sharp contrast with *simillima* line 391, identical twins but very different treatment.

395. **te...quaerit**: 'your severed right hand (*decisa dextera*), Larides, searched for you, its owner (*te suum*)'.

396. **semianimes**: with *digiti*; note the scansion – *sēmianimes*, the first 'i' is treated as a consonant. **micant**: Virgil's choice of this verb must allude to the expression *digitis micare* which describes the game played by children in which they suddenly put up a number of fingers for their opponent to guess.

397. Take *mixtus...armat* before *Arcadas*.

398. **viri**: 'of their hero', with both *monitu* and *facta*. **mixtus...pudor**: 'a mixture of remorse and shame'.

399. **praeter**: adv. with *fugientem*, 'flying past'. **Rhoetea**: Greek acc. of Rhoeteus, cf. *Cissea* line 317.

400. **hoc...Ilo**: *Ilo* is dat., 'Ilus had this breathing-space and this much respite'. Note the striking repetition of *Ilo* emphasising the short duration of the respite.

401. **Ilo namque procul derexerat**: 'for it was at Ilus in the distance that he had aimed'.

402. **quam**: i.e. Pallas' spear. Rhoeteus had been fleeing from Teuthras and Tyres when he was struck in the middle of his body by Pallas' spear.

405. **optato**: a single-word abl. absol. used adverbially, lit. 'it having been prayed for', i.e. 'in accordance with his wish'.

406. **dispersa...incendia**: 'sets fire to the woods here and there'; *silvis* is dat.

407. **una**: 'continuous'.

408. *horrida* and *Volcania* both agree with *acies*; **acies Volcania**: 'a line of fire'.

409. This line helps to relate the simile to the fighting: *victor*, the shepherd in the simile, represents the victorious Pallas. Note the use of military words towards the end of the simile, e.g. *acies* and *ovantes*.

410. **non aliter**: 'in the same way'. **socium**: gen. pl. **coit in unum**: this phrase refers back to *extenditur una* line 407.

411. **bellis acer Halaesus**: a descriptive phrase very like those commonly found in Homer. **bellis**: *in* omitted, 'in war'.

412. **seque...arma**: lit. 'and collected himself into his armour', i.e. 'and

concealed himself behind his shield'.

413. **Ladona, Phereta**: both Greek acc., of Ladon and Pheres. None of these three men is mentioned elsewhere in the poem.

414. **Strymonio dextram**: 'Strymonius' right hand'.

415. **elatam in iugulum**: 'raised (to grasp) his throat'.

417. **fata canens**: a descriptive phrase, 'a prophet'. **silvis**: 'in the woods'. **celarat**: for *celaverat*.

419. Halaesus is described here as a sacrificial victim killed by the Fates through their agent Pallas. **iniecere**: for *iniecerunt*. **sacrarunt**: for *sacraverunt*, 'they consecrated him by Evander's weapons.'

420. **sic**: with *precatus* and referring to the next line.

421. **da ferro quod missile libro**: *libro* is a verb here, 'grant to my weapon which I brandish for a throw'. Note scansion of voc. *Thȳbri̯*.

423. Prayers were often accompanied by vows to be fulfilled later. For trees decorated with arms cf. Bk. XI 5-6.

424. **texit**: 'protected'. **Imaona**: Greek acc. of Imaon.

425. **Arcadio**: Pallas' father Evander according to legend had migrated from Arcadia in Greece to Italy. **dat**: 'he exposed'. **inermum**: group 2 adj. here, though normally group 3.

426. **tanta**: with *caede*. **viri**: gen. sing. referring to Pallas. **non perterrita sinit agmina**: 'did not allow his forces (to be) terrified'. Lausus, the son of Mezentius, was described in Bk. VII as deserving a better father.

427. **pars ingens belli**: supply *est*, 'who played a great part in the war'. **Abantem**: on Abas see line 170.

428. **pugnae...moramque**: a description of Abas, 'a block and impediment in the battle'; Virgil may have been thinking of a knot (*nodum*) in a piece of timber that hinders the axe.

430. **Grais**: dat. of the agent. **Grais imperdita**: 'unscathed by the Greeks'; i.e. those Trojans who escaped from the Trojan War.

432. **extremi**: 'those in the rear'.

433. **hinc...hinc**: 'on this side...on that'.

434. **contra**: adv.

435. **egregii**: pl. adj. describing Pallas and Lausus. **quis**: for *quibus*. **negarat**: for *negaverat*.

436f. **reditus**: acc. pl. 'homecomings'. **passus**: from *patior*, supply *est*;

subject of this verb is *regnator* line 437. Take *tamen* first and put *haud* with *passus*.

438. Pallas is killed by Turnus (line 479) and Lausus by Aeneas (line 815).

439. **alma soror**: i.e. Juturna, sister of Turnus.

441. **tempus**: supply *est*. **pugnae**: probably dat. rather than gen., see line 50.

442. **ego...feror**: *ego* is emphatic, 'It is I who am going against Pallas'. **Pallanta**: see note to line 374. Note the emphatic repetition of *solus... soli* and *ego... mihi*.

443. **cuperem**: 'I would like'; supply *ut* before *ipse*. **parens**: 'his parent' not 'my parent'. **spectator**: 'as a spectator', 'to watch'. The savage character of Turnus and his attack on Pallas is clearly portrayed by the poet. Here Turnus wishes Pallas' aged father could watch the attack; at line 491 he strips Pallas of his belt which is to have important repercussions in Book XII; at line 500 his arrogant boasting is excessive. The killing of Patroclus by Hector in the *Iliad* can be compared with this killing of Pallas. There the result is that Achilles returns to avenge Patroclus by killing Hector, here Aeneas in Book XII dismisses Turnus' pleas for mercy and kills him.

444. **aequore...iusso**: abl. absol., 'when an open space had been ordered'.

445. **Rutulum**: gen. pl. **iuvenis**: i.e. Pallas. Note the arrogance of Turnus is stressed by *superba* and *tyranni* line 448.

447. **obitque...visu**: 'and at a distance surveyed all of him with a stern gaze'.

448. **it contra**: 'he answered'. **dicta**: since Turnus has not spoken yet, this must refer, like *iussa* in line 445, to his order to clear a space (line 444).

449. Turnus expects to be praised either for killing his enemy and taking his armour as spoils (*raptis spoliis*) or for dying gloriously (*leto insigni*).

450. **aequus**: i.e. 'equally ready for', with dat. **sorti...est**: this remark answers Turnus' cruel wish in line 443.

451. **tolle minas**: 'away with your threats'. **fatus**: from *for*.

453. **pedes**: adj. 'on foot', describing Turnus.

454. **utque leo:** 'and like a lion'; the simile of the lion matches that describing Hector as he moves in to finish off the wounded Patroclus in *Iliad* Book XVI.

455. **campis:** for *in campis*. **meditantem in proelia:** 'practising for battle'. **taurum:** in the *Iliad* Patroclus is likened to a wild boar.

456. **imago:** i.e. 'the sight of'.

457. **hunc:** i.e. Turnus. **contiguum missae hastae:** 'near enough for a spear cast'.

458f. **ire:** an historic infin., 'he advanced first'. **si...imparibus:** 'to see if chance would favour him (*fors adiuvet*) making a daring move (*ausum*) though with inferior strength'. **qua:** 'in some way'.

459. **aethera:** Greek acc. sing. of *aether* going with *magnum*.

460. **advena:** 'as a visitor'.

461. **Alcide:** voc. of Alcides, see note to line 321. The hospitality referred to was offered by Evander to Hercules on his way back from Spain, see Bk. VIII line 362. Supply *ut* after *precor* to introduce *adsis*.

462. **cernat semineci sibi:** 'may he (Turnus) see...from him when at the point of death'; *sibi* is dat. of deprivation, 'from him'; cf. dat. after *adimo*.

463. **victoremque ferant:** 'endure (to see) their conqueror'.

465. **inanes:** note the emphatic position of this word. Hercules knew that Pallas was doomed even before Jupiter told him.

466. **genitor:** i.e. Jupiter. **natum:** i.e. Hercules. **amicis:** an adj. here.

467. **stat...dies:** 'for each man (*cuique*) his own day (*sua dies*) stands fixed'. The initial monosyllable emphasises the immutability of fate. *Dies* is usually m., but when it means a particular day it is f., as here.

467-9. The heroic view of life.

469. **hoc opus:** supply *est*, 'this is the task of...'.

470. **cecidere:** for *ceciderunt*, from *cado*. **deum:** gen. pl. **quin:** = *quin etiam*, 'yes, even'. **una:** adv. 'with them'.

472. **dati:** i.e. allotted to him by the fates.

473. **reicit oculos:** 'he turned his eyes away from'. Jupiter turns his eyes away because he is powerless to intervene.

476. **illa:** i.e. the spear thrown by Pallas. **umeri...summa:** 'where the top of the shoulder's protection juts up'.

477.   **viam...per oras:** 'forcing its way (*viam molita*) through the rim of the shield'.

478.   **etiam:** 'actually'. **strinxit de:** 'grazed'.

479.   **robur:** 'a shaft of oak'.

481.   **mage:** old form of *magis*. **nostrum:** 'my'. **penetrabile:** here active in meaning, 'piercing'.

482-5.   A complex sentence; the subject is *cuspis*, the object *clipeum* and the first verb *transverberat*. **terga:** 'layers', repeat *terga* with *aeris*.

483.   **totiens circumdata:** 'wrapped round so many times'. **obeat:** subj. with concessive force, **quem pellis obeat:** 'though a skin covered it'.

484.   **medium:** refers back to *clipeum* in line 482.

485.   **loricaeque moras:** 'the barrier of his breastplate'.

486.   **ille:** i.e. Pallas.

487.   **via:** 'passage', 'route'. Note scansion of *eādem* abl. sing. and *sangūis*.

488.   **super:** adv. 'over him'. **dedere:** for *dederunt*.

489.   **terram petit ore:** 'he hits the ground with his face'.

490.   **super:** with *quem*. The short line perhaps marks a dramatic pause before Turnus violates the body of Pallas.

491.   **haec:** refers to *qualem...remitto* in line 492.

492.   **qualem meruit:** 'in the state he deserved (to have him)'. Evander, according to Turnus, deserved to have his son returned to him dead because he gave Aeneas hospitality and military help. **Pallanta:** see note to line 374.

493.   Take *est* in both clauses. **solamen humandi:** 'consolation in burying (him)'.

494.   **largior:** a verb, not a comparative adj. **haud...hospitia:** 'his hospitality to Aeneas (*hospitia Aeneia*) will cost him dear'. Take *haud* with *parvo*, an abl. of price.

496.   **baltei:** the belt is heavy (*immania pondera*) with metal facings engraved with mythical scenes. It is this belt that will ultimately cost Turnus his life at the hands of Aeneas (Bk. XII 941ff.). This is why it is described in such detail here.

497.   **impressumque nefas:** 'and its engraved (scene of) wickedness'. The picture concerned the marriage of the 50 sons of Aegyptus to the 50 daughters of Danaus. On the insistence of their father all

the brides except one murdered their bridegrooms.

498. **manus:** 'a band'. **foede:** adv., take with *caesa*, 'foully slain'.

499. **quae:** n. pl., 'things which'.

500. **quo spolio:** 'at this spoil'.

501. **nescia:** supply *est; nescia* is followed by two constructions (1) by genitives *fati mortisque* 'of fate and destiny', (2) by the infinitive *servare* 'how to preserve moderation'. Note how Virgil breaks into the narrative with this comment on the behaviour of people when swept away by success.

502. **sublata:** from *tollo.*

503. **magno...Pallanta:** literally 'when he will have wished that un-injured Pallas had been bought at a great price', i.e. 'when he would have paid anything not to have harmed Pallas'.

504. **ista:** agrees with *spolia*, but applies also to *diem.*

505. Note how Virgil emphasises Turnus' future hatred (*oderit*) of what he has just achieved with such exultation (*ovat*).

506. **impositum referunt:** = *imponunt et referunt.*

507. The poet intervenes once more to address Pallas. **o...parenti:** 'O you who will return (*rediture*) as a great grief and glory to your father'. **magnum:** with both nouns.

508. Note the unusual elision immediately after the fifth foot.

509. **cum tamen:** 'and yet'. **ingentes...acervos:** 'great heaps of Rutulian dead'.

510. **fama:** supply *erat.* **certior auctor:** 'a more trustworthy informant'.

511. **tenui...suos:** 'that his men were within a hair's breadth of destruction'. This clause and the following one are acc. + infin. as *advolat Aeneae* is tantamount to *dixit Aeneae.*

512. **tempus:** supply *esse*, 'and that it was time'.

513. **proxima...metit:** 'he mowed down everything around him'. **latum:** more likely describing *limitem* than *agmen.* The imagery is that of harvesting – *metit*, continued by *limitem* 'a swathe' and *ferro* 'a blade'.

515. **caede nova:** with *superbum*, 'arrogant from your recent slaughter'; the *nova caede* refers to the slain Pallas. **Pallas, Euander...:** the broken opening of this sentence underlines Aeneas' agitation. **in ipsis oculis:** 'before his very eyes'.

516. **omnia:** 'the whole scene'. **primas:** Evander had been the first person in Italy to welcome Aeneas.

517. **dextrae:** 'welcome' or 'pledges'. **Sulmone, Ufens:** there is some debate whether Sulmo is a town or a man and Ufens a river or another man. Sulmo, the Rutulian, appears in Book IX and Ufens is mentioned as a member of the Italian forces in Book VII. Perhaps we should assume that the two names indicate people. **Sulmone creatos:** 'sons of Sulmo'.

518. **hic:** 'then'. **totidem:** i.e. four.

519. **quos:** here + subj. to indicate purpose. **inferias...umbris:** 'as an offering to the shades'. In the *Iliad* Achilles plans to sacrifice twelve Trojan young men to the ghost of his dead friend Patroclus.

521. **Mago:** dat. for the more usual *in Magum*, 'at Magus'.

522. **subit:** 'he ducked'.

524. Magus appeals to Aeneas as a son and father – appropriately since he goes on to refer to his own father and son.

525. **precor:** supply *ut* to introduce *serves*.

526. Magus is suggesting that Aeneas might accept money to allow him to live. **est:** supply *mihi*.

527f. **facti infecti:** 'worked', 'unworked'; i.e. 'in coins', 'not in coins'.

528. **non...vertitur:** 'the Trojans' victory does not depend on this'. **hic:** 'here', i.e. whether Magus is spared or not. **Teucrum:** gen. pl.

529. **anima...tanta:** 'one life will not make such a great difference'. **discrimina tanta:** acc. pl. for sing.

530. **cui contra:** *contra* is adv., 'to whom in reply'.

531. Note the word order here; Aeneas raises Magus' hopes by mentioning the money first only to dash them with *natis parce tuis*. **memoras...talenta:** 'the many talents which you mention'.

532. **natis tuis:** 'for your children'. **belli...ista:** 'Turnus has destroyed those bargains in war'.

533. **prior iam:** with *sustulit*. **tum:** 'at that moment when'.

534. Supply *sentiunt* from *sentit* to go with *manes*. This line specifically answers Magus' plea of line 524.

535. **laeva:** abl. sing.

536. **capulo tenus:** 'up to the hilt'; *tenus* regularly follows its noun.

537. **nec procul:** supply a verb, such as *aberat*.

538. **cui:** with *tempora*, 'whose temples'. *infula* is nom., *sacra vitta* are abl. This line shows how scansion helps in translation.

539. **albis:** also describing *veste*.
540. **quem:** i.e. Haemonides. **campo:** 'over the plain'.
541. **immolat:** a religious word, see line 519, i.e. he was despatched like a victim.
542. **lecta refert:** 'he gathered up (*lecta* from *lego*) and brought back'. **umeris:** for *in umeris*. **tibi tropaeum:** 'as a trophy for you'.
543. **instaurant:** subjects are Caeculus and Umbro in line 544. **Volcani...creatus:** 'born from the family of Vulcan'.
544. **montibus:** for *ex montibus*.
545. **Dardanides:** i.e. Aeneas. **ense:** 'with his sword'. Aeneas cuts off the left arm of Anxur which was holding his shield. Anxur, like other victims of Aeneas which follow – Tarquitus, Antaeus, Lucas, Numa, Niphaeus and Lucagus – is not known elsewhere.
546. **ferro:** i.e. the *ense* of line 545, 'with his sword'.
547. **ille:** i.e. Anxur. **aliquid magnum:** 'something boastful'. **vim... verbo:** 'there would be (*adfore* = *adfuturam esse*) force (i.e. to match) his talk'.
548. **caeloque...ferebat:** lit. 'perhaps he was raising his spirit to the sky', i.e. 'perhaps he was carried away by a soaring ambition'. **caelo:** dat., for *in caelum*.
551. **quem:** to be taken at the beginning of the line. **crearat:** for *creaverat*, 'whom she had borne for...'.
552. **ardenti:** describes Aeneas, and is dat. after obvius. **ille:** i.e. Aeneas. **reducta hasta:** 'drew back (and threw) his spear'.
553. **impedit:** 'he obstructed', i.e. 'he pierced'.
555. **deturbat terrae:** 'he lopped off on to the ground'. **terrae:** dat. for the more usual *in terram*, see *Mago* line 521. Note the heavy alliteration in this line.
556. **super:** adv. 'over him'.
557. Note the bitter sarcasm of *metuende* and *optima*.
558. **humi:** locative. **patrioque...sepulcro:** supply *non* from previous line.
559. **linquere:** for *linqueris*, 'you will be left'. **mersum:** from *mergo*, supply *te*.
561. **prima agmina:** i.e. Antaeus and Lucas, 'Turnus' front line'.
562. **fulvum:** refers to the colour of Camers' hair.
563. **satum:** from *sero*, 'sprung from', i.e. 'son of'. **ditissimus:** followed

by the gen., 'very rich in land'.

564. **qui:** refers to *Volcente* in previous line. **Ausonidum:** with *ditissimus*, 'richest of the Italians'. Amyclae was a town in Latium reputedly named after Amyclae in Laconia from where it was said to have been colonised. **tacitis:** Servius records that after numerous false reports of invading forces, a law was passed that no one was to report the arrival of the enemy; consequently it was captured.

565. This simile stresses the primeval, superhuman savagery of Aeneas' onslaught. **Aegaeon:** another name for Briareus, the giant with a hundred arms. **cui:** supply *esse*. **dicunt:** 'people say'.

566. **centenasque:** the distributive numeral is used again for the cardinal, see line 329. **ignem arsisse:** '(and) fire blazed out from', *arsisse* after *dicunt*.

567. **contra:** with *fulmina Iovis*.

568. **paribus:** 'matching'.

569. **desaevit:** 'rampaged'.

570. **ut...mucro:** 'when once the point of his sword grew warm'.

571. **adversa pectora:** i.e. Aeneas rushed at the horses head-on.

572. **illi:** 'they', subject, i.e. the horses. Take *ut videre*, i.e. *ut viderunt* before *longe gradientem*; supply *eum*, i.e. Aeneas, to *gradientem* and *frementem*.

573f. Note how the short phrases correspond to the speed of the events. **ducem:** 'owner'. **currus:** for *currum* the singular.

575. **biiugis:** a two-horse chariot, ridden by Lucagus and Liger.

576. **in medios:** 'into the thick of the fray'.

577. **rotat:** i.e. Lucagus was swinging his sword in wide arcs. **acer:** almost an adv.

578. **tanto fervore:** with *furentes*.

579. **adversa hasta:** scansion will show that this is an abl. phrase.

580. **cui:** supply *dixit*.

581. In the *Iliad* Aeneas was rescued from Diomedes by Aphrodite and from Achilles by Poseidon. **Achilli:** genitive.

582. **finis:** with *belli* and *aevi*. **aevi:** 'of your life'.

583. **his terris:** for *in his terris*.

584. **Ligeri:** dat., 'from Liger'. **et:** 'too'.

585. **contra:** adv., 'in reply'.

586.   pronus...verbera: 'bending forward to (apply) the lash'. **telo**: 'with the flat of his sword'.

588.   aptat se pugnae: 'was getting himself ready for the fight', i.e. for his encounter with Aeneas. **subit**: this compound emphasises the sudden unexpected arrival of the spear; it is related to the adv. *subito*.

590.   arvis: for *in arvis*, 'on the ground'.

591.   pius: here used ironically by the poet, cf. note to line 604. **amaris**: from *amarus* 'bitter' not *amo*.

592.   nulla fuga segnis equorum: 'no sluggish flight of horses'. **tuos currus**: for *tuum currum* the singular.

593.   vertere ex hostibus: *vertere* for *verterunt*, supply *eos*; 'turned your horse away from the enemy'.

594.   rotis saliens: *rotis* for *ex rotis*, 'jumping from (your) chariot'.

595.   frater: i.e. Liger. **inertes**: 'powerless', (a) because he held no weapons and (b) because his prayer to Aeneas will achieve nothing.

597.   Note the grammatical order of words – *per te, per parentes qui...* **genuere**: for *genuerunt*, from *gigno*.

598.   sine: 'spare', literally 'leave alone'. **misereor** regularly takes the gen. **precantis**: supply *mei*.

599.   pluribus: supply *verbis*. **oranti**: supply *ei dixit*.

600.   dabas: 'you were uttering'. Note the hard-hitting alliteration of 'd'. **morere**: imperative of *morior*. **ne desere**: a neg. command, 'don't desert'.

601.   latebras animae: 'the hiding-place of his life breath'; describing *pectus*.

604.   more: with the gen., 'in the manner of', 'like'. **furens**: this word summarises Aeneas' mood during the last few incidents; his actions and behaviour have been marked by a lack of control.

605.   obsessa: describing *iuventus*.

608.   rebare: for *rebaris*.

609f. non vivida...viris: 'not their men's (*viris*) right arms (*dextra*) active in the war (*vivida bello*)'; this comment by Jupiter is ironic since Aeneas' recent exploits clearly demonstrate the power of Trojan men in war. **patiensque pericli**: 'nor their ability to endure danger'. The shortening of a word such as *pericli* is called 'syncope'.

611. **cui**: supply *dixit*. **o...coniunx**: there is a hint of sarcasm in this.
612. **sollicitas**: 'you taunt'. Note the bitter alliteration of 't' in this line. **aegram...timentem**: supply *me*.
613. **quae...decebat**: 'which it once had, and rightly so', *quae* and *quam* refer to *vis* in line 614.
614. **vis in amore foret**: with *si mihi*; **foret** = *esset*, 'if there were influence in my love'. **namque**: emphatic, 'then'. **non hoc mihi negares quin**: 'you would not deny me this that...', followed by *possem* in line 616.
615. **pugnae**: dat., cf. line 50.
616. **Dauno**: dat. with *parenti*, 'for his father Daunus'.
617. A bitterly angry line; note the use of *pio*. Juno is suggesting that Turnus is just as worthy as Aeneas. **pereat...det**: 'let him perish and pay'. **Teucris**: dative.
618. **ille**: i.e. Turnus.
619. In line 76 Pilumnus was Turnus' grandfather, here his great-great-grandfather. **tua**: with *limina*. **larga**: with *manu*. Juno is giving examples of Turnus' alleged *pietas*, cf. *pio* in line 617.
622. **mora praesentis leti**: 'delay in death that is close at hand'.
623. **meque...sentis**: 'and you realise that I ordain this so'; *hoc* refers to Turnus' fate to be killed by Aeneas.
624. **eripe**: supply *Turnum* from earlier in the line.
625. **hactenus...vacat**: 'I am permitted to indulge (you) this far'; supply *mihi* with *vacat*. **altior venia**: 'a more far-reaching favour'.
626. **latet**: 'lurks'. **moveri**: 'be influenced'.
628. **Iuno**: supply *dixit*. **quae voce...mente dares**: 'you were to grant in your mind (*mente dares*) what you begrudge to say openly (*quae voce gravaris*)'.
629. **Turno rata maneret**: 'were to remain assured for Turnus'.
630. **nunc**: see note to line 617. **insontem**: supply *eum*. Juno sees that Turnus is facing death. **aut...feror**: 'or I am carried away devoid of truth'.
631. **quod ut o potius ludar**: 'but how I would rather be deluded'. *quod ut* is like *quod si*. **ludar**: pres. subj. for a wish.
632. **in melius reflectas**: *reflectas* is pres. subj. like *ludar*, 'you would alter for the better'. **orsa**: 'intentions'.
633. **caelo alto**: for *e caelo alto*.

634. **nimbo**: goes closely with *succincta*, 'shrouded in a cloud'.
636. Supply a verb like 'fashioned' to the nom. *dea*. **nube cava**: 'from a hollow cloud'. **sine viribus**: either 'effortlessly' describing Juno, or 'without substance' describing the phantom. The words in this line – *nube...umbram* emphasise the phantom's lack of substance. In the *Iliad* Apollo made a phantom in the form of Aeneas after he had removed Aeneas from the battle.
637. **visu mirabile**: 'remarkable to see'.
639. **divini capitis**: with *iubas*, 'the crests of his divine head'; i.e. Aeneas as born of a goddess. **inania verba**: 'meaningless words'.
640. **sine mente sonum**: 'sound without intelligence', possibly like a robot as suggested by Page. **gressus euntis**: 'his steps as he walked'.
641. **quales fama est figuras**: 'like the ghosts (*quales figuras*) that are commonly believed (*fama est*)'. This line refers to the ghosts of the dead, the next to figures that appear in dreams.
642. **somnia quae**: 'dreams which...'. **sensus**: acc. pl.
643. Juno's creation is unlike the traditional ghosts and phantoms which were grim and gloomy.
644. **virum**: i.e. Turnus.
645. **cui**: a delayed connecting relative.
646. **illa**: = *imago*.
647f. **ut Turnus credidit**: 'when Turnus believed that'. **Aenean**: see note to line 65.
648. **animo...inanem**: 'in his disturbed state (*turbidus*) seized on the empty hope (*spem hausit inanem*) in his mind'.
649. **thalamos**: 'marriage'. **ne desere**: see note to line 600. Aeneas was betrothed to Lavinia, daughter of king Latinus; previously Lavinia had been betrothed to Turnus.
650. **tellus...per undas**: 'the land you sought for over the sea'. Supply *tibi* to *dabitur*. This line is a bitter double-entendre; Aeneas looked for a new land, Turnus offers him a grave.
652. **nec...ventos**: 'and does not see the winds carrying away his joyful (expectations)'. Servius says that *venti ferunt gaudia* was a proverb.
653. **ratis...saxi**: 'a ship joined to (*ratis coniuncta*) a quay (*crepidine*) of a high rock'. *coniunctus* more usually takes dat. or *cum* + abl.
654. **ponte**: 'gangway', see line 288.

655. **advectus:** supply *erat*. **oris:** for *ex oris*.

656. **huc:** i.e. to the ship.

657. **in latebras:** i.e. 'to hide'. **nec segnior:** 'and no slower', i.e. 'equally quickly'.

658. **moras:** 'obstacles'.

660. 'and bore the ship off (*rapit navem*) swept away (*avulsam*) over the ebbing waters'.

661. This and the following line describes what is happening in the meantime on the battlefield. **illum:** i.e. Turnus. **in proelia:** note the acc., 'for battle'.

662. **obvia:** transferred epithet, i.e. really 'bodies of men in his way'. **virum:** gen. pl.

663. **levis:** with *imago*.

664. **sublime:** adv. 'up into the sky'. **se immiscuit:** 'evaporated into', + dat.

665. **cum interea:** 'while all this time'. **medio aequore:** 'over the middle of the sea', i.e. 'out to sea'.

666. **ignarus rerum:** 'unaware of his plight'. **ingratusque salutis:** the gen. after *ingratus* is very rare but is helped by the preceding phrase, 'unappreciative of his deliverance'.

667. **cum voce:** i.e. 'as he spoke'.

668. **tanton:** for *tantone*; **tanto crimine:** abl. after *dignum*.

669. **duxisti:** 'did you consider?'. **voluisti:** supply *me* from previous line.

670. Two questions have been run together. Turnus is even unsure of his identity as he finds himself running away from an enemy. **quae...reducit:** 'what flight (*quae fuga*) takes me away (*me ducit*)? Whom does it bring back?' Supply *ducit* from *reducit* to *quae fuga*.

672. **quid manus illa virum:** 'what about that band of men?' **virum:** gen. pl. **secuti:** supply *sunt*.

673. **quosne:** the *-ne* is for emphasis and is not translated. **nefas:** an exclamation 'what a crime'.

674. Turnus has a vision of his men wandering about and some being killed (*cadentum*); **cadentum:** for *cadentium*.

675. **accipio:** a shortened poetic version of *accipio ad aures*, 'I hear'. **quid ago?:** pres. tense for more usual deliberative subj. 'what am I to do?' **satis ima:** 'sufficiently deeply'. **dehiscat:** subj. 'would gape open'.

676. **o potius:** an exclamation, see line 631. **miserescite:** supply *mei*.
677. **volens:** 'gladly'; the alliteration emphasises that Turnus is praying for his own destruction. **vos:** i.e. the winds Turnus is praying to.
678. **saevis vadis:** dat. 'on to the savage shallows'. **Syrtis:** gen. sing.
679. **quo:** 'where'. **conscia fama:** 'any rumour of my disgrace'. **sequatur:** subj. because it is a virtual purpose clause.
681f. **sese induat:** 'he should cast himself upon'; a very unusual use of *induo* + abl., we would expect *induo in* + acc. or *induo* + dat. Virgil appears to be treating it as if it meant 'transfix'.
683. **iaciat:** supply *sese* from line 681. **fluctibus:** dat. for *in fluctus*. **nando:** gerund, 'by swimming'.
684. **Teucrum in arma:** 'to the battle with the Trojans'. **Teucrum:** gen. pl.
685. **utramque viam:** 'each course of action', i.e. suicide or a return to battle.
686. **animi:** locative. **animi miserata:** 'pitying him in her heart'.
687. **labitur:** subject is the ship. **alta:** n. pl., 'the high sea'. **secundo:** with both *fluctu* and *aestu*.
688. **urbem:** Ardea, a city of Latium.
689. **Iovis monitis:** perhaps Jupiter encouraged Mezentius to bring about his well-deserved downfall or Mezentius was urged on to compensate for the absence of Turnus. Mezentius, formerly ruler of the Etruscans, had been expelled by his people because of his violent behaviour and had taken refuge with Turnus.
691f. **omnibus...instant:** 'with all their hatred (*omnibus odiis*) and massed weapons (*telis frequentibus*) they pressed upon the one lone man'. Note the striking juxtaposition of *omnibus uni* and the repetition of *uni* for strong emphasis.
694. **exposta:** = *exposita*, by syncope.
696. The simile ends with *manens* and *ille* i.e. Mezentius takes over. **Hebrum:** unknown elsewhere in the *Aeneid* as also are Latagus, Palmus, Euanthes and Mimas.
697. **humi:** locative, 'on the ground'. **cum quo:** supply *sternit*.
698. **saxo...montis:** a hendiadys, 'with a massive boulder broken from a mountain'.
699. **os faciemque adversam:** a second object along with *Latagum* describing the part actually attacked. Homer employs a similar

construction quite commonly. **poplite succiso**: abl. absol.

700. **volvi segnem**: 'to roll about crippled'. **arma ...umeris**: 'he gave the armour to Lausus to wear (*habere*) on his shoulders'. **umeris et vertice**: for *in umeris et in vertice*.

702. **nec non**: these cancel out, 'and furthermore'. **Euanthen, Mimanta**: Greek accusatives; supply *sternit* from line 697.

703f. **una nocte et**: 'on the same night as'. **Theano in lucem dedit**: 'Theano gave to the light of day', i.e. 'Theano gave birth to'.

705. **Cisseis regina**: 'the daughter of Cisseus, the queen'; supply *in lucem dedit* from line 704. Before Paris was born, Hecuba, the queen, dreamt that she was giving birth to a firebrand. **urbe paterna**: for *in urbe paterna*.

706. **ignarum**: 'but where, no one knows'. Death and burial away from one's family and homeland was considered a great tragedy. **Mimanta**: see note to line 702.

707. **ac velut ille aper**: 'and he like a boar', i.e. Mezentius. **canum morsu**: 'by snapping dogs'.

709. **defendit**: perf. tense rather than pres. **-que palus Laurentia**: supply *defendit*, 'or (*-que*) one which the Laurentine marsh has defended'; the poet is clearly describing a second boar in a different area. **multos**: supply *annos*. **silva...harundinea**: 'fed on the reedy vegetation'.

710. **ventum est**: impersonal passive for *venit* (*aper*).

711. **armos**: 'across his shoulders', lit. 'as to his shoulders' acc. of respect.

712. **nec cuiquam virtus**: supply *erat*, 'nor did anyone have the courage'; *irasci* is at first sight an unusual verb to apply to the hunters, but since the boar represents Mezentius, just as the Etruscans were furious at Mezentius for his past brutality so the hunters were angry with the boar, presumably because of its depredations.

713. Some editors read lines 717 and 718 after this line and apply them to the boar. But there is no manuscript authority for doing so and secondly, as Page and others point out, these lines would then repeat line 711.

714f. **iustae irae**: a predicative dat.; to *quibus* and *non ulli* (line 715) supply *eorum* as the antecedent, 'not one of those (*non ulli eorum*) who had (*quibus est*) a just cause for anger against Mezentius (*iustae Mezentius irae*) had the courage to (*est animus*)...'.

716. Supply *eum* after *lacessunt*.
717. **partes...omnes**: 'turns slowly in all directions'.
718. **tergo**: presumably 'from his shield'. I know of no other use of this word on its own to mean 'shield'; in line 482 *terga* is used for 'layers' and *clipeum* is used with it; see also line 784.
719. Acron does not appear anywhere else in the poem.
721. **hunc**: i.e. Acron. The subject of *vidit* is Mezentius. **miscentem media agmina**: 'causing confusion in the thick of the battle'.
722. **pactae coniugis ostro**: presumably some kind of purple garment given to him by his beloved. Ovid twice in his *Amores* describes *amor* as *purpureus*.
723. **impastus leo ceu**: 'like a starving lion'. **stabula alta**: 'high-sided pens'. **saepe**: 'as often happens'. Another simile of a wild animal to describe Mezentius. This simile along with that in line 707ff. is very reminiscent of Homeric epic style and the *Iliad* in particular. They emphasise Mezentius as a rugged hero like Ajax or Diomede.
725. **aut...cervum**: 'or a towering antlered stag'; lit. 'or a stag towering up to his antlers'. This phrase is in sharp contrast with *fugacem capream*.
726. **immane**: adv. **haeret**: 'pounces'.
727. **incumbens**: 'throwing himself on'.
732. **idem**: i.e. Mezentius. Orodes does not appear elsewhere in the poem.
733. **caecum**: 'unseen', i.e. a wound in the back.
734. **obvius...occurrit**: 'he runs to block his path (*obvius*) and meet him head-on (*adverso*)'. **viro vir**: 'man to man'.
735. **haud**: with *furto*. **haud...armis**: 'a better man not by stealth but by prowess in arms'.
736. **tum...hasta**: 'then with his foot placed (*posito pede*) on the fallen man (*super abiectum*) and leaning on his spear (*nixus et hasta*)'.
737. **pars**: see note to line 427. **haud temnenda**: 'not to be despised'. **viri**: voc. pl. We should imagine that Mezentius is addressing his own men. See *socii* in the next line. **iacet altus**: note the emphatic juxtaposition.

738. **paeana:** Greek acc. **paeana secuti:** 'following his cry of triumph'.

739. **ille:** i.e. Orodes. **non me inulto:** abl. absol., i.e. 'I will not be unavenged'.

740. **longum:** 'for long'. **laetabere:** for *laetaberis*.

741. Supply *te* from the previous line to go with *tenebis*.

742. **ad quae:** supply a verb of speaking. **subridens:** *sub-* suggests a sneer rather than a smile.

743. **morere:** sing. imperat. of *morior*. **ast...viderit:** 'but as for me (*ast de me*) let the father of the gods and king of men see to it'. **viderit:** perf. subj. for a wish. This must be a sarcastic remark, see note to line 773f.

745. **olli:** archaic spelling of *illi*, dat. sing. **olli oculos:** 'his eyes'. Note how the remorseless manner of his death is emphasised by the two adjs. – *dura* and *ferreus*. This description of death has been modelled on Homer.

747f. These lines list Latin successes over Trojans, some of whom have Greek sounding names with the Greek acc. form: e.g. *Hydaspen*. Messapus is the only one to be mentioned elsewhere in the poem; see line 354. Supply *obtruncat* to each subject.

749. **Lycaonium:** 'son of Lycaon'.

750. **illum:** 'the former', i.e. Clonius. **infrenis equi:** gen. phrase after *lapsu* 'after a fall from his horse ridden without reins'. **tellure:** for *in tellure*.

751. **hunc:** 'the latter', i.e. Ericaetes. **pedes:** nom. sing. of adj. 'on foot', describing Agis.

753. Supply *deicit* to *Salius* and *Nealces*. **Salius Saliumque:** Virgil is trying to describe a rapid series of exchanges producing deaths on both sides; no sooner has Salius killed than he is killed himself.

754. **longe fallente:** with *sagitta* 'deceiving from a long distance'.

755. **gravis:** with *Mavors*, 'grim Mars'.

757. Supply *erat* to **fuga nota**.

758. **inanem:** the gods knew that for all their anger and efforts mortals were unable to change what is fixed by fate.

759. **et mortalibus esse:** 'and that mortals had'.

761. **Tisiphone media inter milia:** 'Tisiphone in the middle between the (warring) thousands'. Tisiphone was one of the Erinyes or Furies, who tormented those who violated the laws of society.

763. **turbidus:** 'like a whirlwind'. **ingreditur:** 'stalks'. **campo:** for *in campo*. **quam magnus Orion:** 'as tall as Orion', the fourth simile about Mezentius.

764f. **medii...stagna:** 'through the vast waters (*per maxima stagna*) of the middle of the sea'.

766. **summis montibus:** for *de summis montibus*.

767. **solo:** 'on the ground', see *campo* line 763.

768. **armis:** from *armus*, 'with shoulders', not 'with weapons'; see previous two lines.

769. **huic:** dat. after *obvius ire* in line 770.

770. **ille:** i.e. Mezentius.

771. **et...stat:** 'and with his bulk (*mole sua*) stands (motionless)'; the monosyllabic ending emphasises his immovable stance.

772. **satis hastae:** 'enough for (a cast of) a spear'.

773f. **mihi deus:** in apposition to *dextra*. Mezentius, described in Book VII 648 as *contemptor divum*, relies entirely on his own human skill. **dextra...adsint:** 'let my right hand (*dextra*) – the thing I worship (*mihi deus*) – and the weapon that I balance to throw (*et telum quod missile libro*) now aid me'.

774ff. Further indications of Mezentius' contempt for the gods; he vows to give Aeneas' arms to his son instead of dedicating them to a god. **voveo...Aeneae:** 'I vow that you yourself (*voveo te ipsum*), Lausus, will be dressed in the spoils (*indutum spoliis*) torn from the body of the plunderer (*praedonis corpore raptis*), as a trophy of Aeneas'. The Latins considered Aeneas a plunderer as he had come to settle in their land with, as they felt, no right to do so.

777. **clipeo est excussa:** 'was knocked aside by his shield', i.e. 'glanced off his shield'.

778. Antores is not mentioned elsewhere in the poem. For - *en* see note to line 747.

780. Evander had migrated from Arcadia in Greece to Pallanteum, a settlement on the river Tiber; we should presume that Antores left his native Argos – called Argi by Virgil – and joined Evander's migration. **Itala urbe:** for *in Itala urbe*.

781. **alieno:** 'meant for someone else'. Note the hypermetric - *que* elided into the next line.

783f. **pius:** in contrast with the character of Mezentius. **per...triplici:**

'through his circular convex shield (*per orbem cavum*) with three layers of bronze (*aere triplici*)'. **terga**: 'layers', see line 482. **tribus tauris**: 'the hides of three bulls'.

785. **ima**: nom., i.e. *ima hasta* 'the point (of the spear)'.
786. **inguine**: for *in inguine*. **sed...pertulit**: 'but it did not carry force (with it)'. Aeneas' spear lost most of its force as it broke through Mezentius' shield.
787. **viso...laetus**: 'happy at the sight of the Etruscan's blood'.
788. **femine**: from *femur*. **trepidanti**: supply *hosti* or *Mezentio*.
789. The sentence begins with Lausus' immediate reaction to the wounding of his father; note the repetition of 'g'.
790. **volutae**: for *volutae sunt*.
791. **casum** and **facta** are both objects of *silebo* in line 793. **mortis... casum**: 'the misfortune of your harsh death'.
792. **si...vetustas**: 'if some antiquity (*si qua vetustas*) is going to confer (*est latura*) credibility (*fidem*) to so great an exploit'.
793. **nec te**: the third object of *silebo* after *casum* and *facta*. Note the emphatic juxtaposition of *memorande* and *silebo*.
794. **ille**: i.e. Mezentius. **inutilis**: 'helpless'. **inque ligatus**: for *inligatusque* or *et inligatus*. The technical word for splitting words in this way is tmesis. Mezentius was hampered by the spear stuck in his shield.
795. **clipeo**: 'with his shield', i.e. 'in his shield'.
796. **sese...armis**: 'involved himself in the battle'.
797ff. **iamque...sustinuit**: 'and he ran under the sword (*subiit mucronem*) of Aeneas as he was lifting his right arm (*Aeneae adsurgentis dextra*) and delivering a blow (*plagamque ferentis*), and checked the hero (*sustinuit ipsum*) with a delaying action (*morando*)'. **dextra**: ablative.
800. **dum**: here + subj. to give the purpose of the action – 'until the father should get away'. Note the juxtaposition of *genitor* and *nati*. **parma**: ablative.
801. **hostem**: i.e. Aeneas.
802. Aeneas' irritation is highlighted by the short phrases and the alliteration of 't'. **-que**: 'but', rather than 'and'.
803. **si quando**: 'whenever'. **effusa**: abl. sing. with *grandine*.
804. **campis**: for *a campis* 'from the plains'.

805. **latet**: 'takes shelter'. **tuta arce**: for *in tuta arce*; *ripis* and *fornice* in line 806 are similar.
806. **amnis ripis**: 'in the (i.e. under the overhanging) banks of a river'.
807. **dum**: 'for as long as'. **sole reducto**: abl. absol.
808. **exercere diem**: 'spend the (rest of the) day at their work'.
809. The simile of the weather is continued in the metaphors of this line; **nubem belli**: 'the storm-cloud of war'. **dum...omnis**: 'until all its thundering should subside'. Note the subj. after *dum*. Supply *nubes* from *nubem* to go with *omnis*.
810. Note the repetition of Lausus' name, i.e. 'Lausus and (only) Lausus'.
811. **maiora viribus**: 'too great for your strength'.
812. **fallit...tua**: rather ironic coming from *pius Aeneas*. **ille**: i.e. Lausus.
813. The intense anger of both men is highlighted by the juxtaposition of *demens* and *saevae*. **saevae...ductori**: 'now the fierce rage of the Trojan leader rose even higher'.
815. **legunt**: 'gather up'; note the ominous word *extrema* in a strong position. The gathering of the threads of life was to prepare for cutting them.
816. **totum**: take this as an adverb.
817f. With two adjectives – *levia...molli* – the poet subtly points out that Lausus was not up to this standard of warfare; see *maiora viribus* in line 811. **levia...minacis**: 'weapons (too) slight for one (so) threatening'.
818. **quam**: refers to *tunicam*.
821. Subject of **vidit** is *Anchisiades* in line 822.
822. **ora**: repeated to add pathos: the use of the patronymic Anchisiades instead of Aeneas subtly anticipates line 824. **modis pallentia miris**: 'growing pale in a strange way'.
823. **graviter**: with *ingemuit*.
824. **patriae pietatis imago**: 'the picture of his love for his father'.
825. **quid tibi**: supply *est*. **pro laudibus istis**: 'for those glorious deeds'.
826. **pius**: echoes *pietatis* in line 824. **tanta indole dignum**: 'worthy of such nobility', lit. 'worthy of so great a temperament'.
827. **laetatus**: for *laetatus es*. **habe**: 'keep'. Aeneas' pity in allowing Lausus to remain in his armour is in sharp contrast with the behaviour of Turnus towards Pallas (491f.). **parentum**:

'ancestors'.

828. **si qua...cura:** 'if that is any concern (to you)'.

829. **hoc:** abl. 'with this' – explained by the following line. **solabere:** for *solaberis*.

830. **ultro:** 'before they did anything'.

831. **socios:** i.e. Lausus' comrades. **terra:** abl. for *a terra*. **ipsum:** i.e. Lausus. Note that Aeneas lifts Lausus' body.

832. **comptos de more:** 'arranged in the customary way'.

833. **genitor:** i.e. Mezentius.

835. **procul:** 'some way off'.

836. **prato:** for *in prato*.

838. **fusus...barbam:** *barbam* is acc. retained in the passive; 'with his flowing beard hanging down on his chest', lit. 'spread out as regards his beard combed forward on his chest'.

840. **qui revocent:** subj. indicates purpose, 'people to recall him'. **maesti:** with *parentis*.

841. The two words *Lausum super* which recall line 839 emphasise the shock that Mezentius is about to receive. Note the word order; Lausus is the focus of attention, so he is placed before *socii*. **super arma:** this phrase echoes the Spartan mother's instruction to her warrior son – 'either (carrying) it or on it'; 'it' was his shield.

842. A line heavy with spondees to match the slow procession.

843. **gemitum:** presumably from the *socii*. **praesaga mali:** 'with a foreboding of evil'. Note the rare monosyllabic ending. **mens:** i.e. of Mezentius.

845. **corpore:** for *in corpore*.

846. **tantane:** a result clause in the form of a question.

847. Supply *te* or *eum* to **paterer** as antecedent to *quem* in line 848. **hostili succedere dextrae:** 'to come under an enemy's right arm'.

848. **tua haec:** with *vulnera*.

849. Note the striking phrase *morte...vivens*.

850. Mezentius feels that his death can only be wretched since his son has died before him and, though Aeneas has wounded him, Lausus' death has made the wound yet deeper. **adactum:** supply *est*.

851f. **idem:** with *ego*. According to the legend followed by Virgil Mezentius was expelled by the Etruscans for his cruel and tyrannical behaviour.

852. **solio...paternis**: supply *e* to both nouns.

853. **meorum**: 'of my people'.

854. **dedissem**: pluperf. subj. – a wish for the past, 'I wish I had given up'. **per**: 'among'.

855. **homines**: '(the world of) men'.

857. **quamquam...tardat**: a very difficult clause, perhaps 'although his strength was failing because of the deep wound'. *Tardat* seems to be used intransitively.

858. **hoc**: nominative, this refers to the horse but has been attracted into the gender of *decus* and *solamen*; supply *erat* from 859, 'this was his glory'.

859. **hoc**: abl., 'on this', lit. 'by this'. Note the build up to the emphatic *omnibus* in line 860.

860. **maerentem**: the horse grieves for its master's pain.

861. **res si...est**: *qua* is fem. sing. of the indefinite *quis*; 'if a long time (*si diu*) is any reality at all (*res qua ulla*) for mortals'.

862. **illa**: i.e. belonging to Aeneas.

864. The heavy beat of the monosyllabic ending reinforces the meaning.

865f. **pariter**: i.e. 'along with me', cf. *mecum* in line 864. **neque enim, credo, pati dignabere**: *neque enim* with *dignabere*, *credo* is in parenthesis, *dignabere* for *dignaberis*; 'for you will not deign to suffer, I believe,...'. **iussa aliena**: 'someone else's orders'.

867. **exceptus tergo**: lit. 'received by its back', i.e. 'mounting on to its back'; *exceptus* suggests that the horse willingly accepted its rider. **consueta**: i.e. accustomed to riding a horse.

869. **caput**: acc. of respect with *fulgens*, lit 'shining as to his head' i.e. 'his head shining with'. **crista equina**: 'with a plume of horse-hair'.

870. **cursum dedit**: 'he set his course'. **in medios**: supply *hostes*.

871. **pudor...luctu**: 'a sense of shame and madness mixed with grief'.

872. This line, found in XII 668, does not fit comfortably here; it is omitted in a number of important manuscripts. **conscia virtus**: 'courage aware of itself'.

873. **Aenean**: see note to line 65.

874. **enim**: 'indeed'.

875. **sic**: explained by the wish in the next line. **pater...deum**: note the

subj. for a wish, 'may that father of the gods'. **altus Apollo**: supply *faciat*. Aeneas is accepting the challenge as the will of the gods.

876.   Supply *ut* to **incipias**, 'that you begin'. **conferre manum**: 'to join battle'.

878.   **ille**: i.e. Mezentius. **erepto nato**: 'since my son has been snatched away', i.e. 'now that you have snatched my son away'.

879.   **terres**: 'you try to frighten'. **haec via**: i.e. the killing of Lausus. **perdere**: supply *me*.

880.   **horremus**: = *horreo*. **parcimus**: = *parco*. **divum**: gen. pl. Mezentius' normal character reasserts itself, after a brief moment of sympathy. The second half of the line recalls an earlier description of him – *contemptor divum*.

883.   **super**: adv. **figit**: the next line makes it clear that he is planting the spears in Aeneas' shield.

885.   **adstantem**: describing Aeneas. **laevos in orbes**: 'in circles to the left'; in that direction Mezentius would have his protected left side facing Aeneas.

887.   **immanem...silvam**: 'carried round in his bronze shield a fearful forest (of spears)'. **tegmine**: for *in tegmine*.

888.   **ubi taedet**: supply *eum*, 'when it wearied him', i.e. 'when he was tired of', followed by the two infinitive phrases.

889.   **urgetur...iniqua**: 'was hard pressed (*urgetur*) since he had engaged (*congressus*) in an unequal fight (*pugna iniqua*)'. Mezentius had an advantage being on his horse.

890.   **multa...animo**: 'turning over many things in his mind'.

892.   **arrectum**: i.e. on its hind legs.

893f.   **effusum...armo** 'and fell itself on top of (*super ipse secutus*) its thrown rider (*effusum equitem*) pinning him down and collapsed (*implicat incumbit*) headfirst with its shoulder out of joint (*cernuus eiecto armo*)'.

895.   **caelum incendunt**: a very vivid phrase, 'set the sky alight'.

896.   **vagina**: ablative.

897.   **super**: adverb, 'standing over him'.

899.   **hausit...recepit**: 'he gulped in air and recovered his senses'. Mezentius had been winded and momentarily stunned by his fall.

900.   **amare**: from *amarus* 'bitter'.

901.   **nullum nefas**: supply *est*. **caede**: Mezentius is referring to his own

death. **sic**: refers back to the previous phrase *nullum...nefas*.

902. **pepigit**: from *pango*, with *foedera*, 'made this bargain'. **mihi**: = *pro me*.

903. **unum hoc oro**: 'this one thing I beg'; *hoc* is explained by the next line. **per**: with *si qua venia* for *per veniam si qua*, 'by mercy, if there is any for'.

904. **corpus**: supply *meum*. **humo**: for *in humo*. **patiare**: for *patiaris*, supply *ut* for indirect command after *oro*, 'that you allow'.

905. **circumstare**: supply *me*. **defende**: 'keep away'. Mezentius feared that his body might be mutilated by his former subjects who now hated him.

906. **me concede**: supply *esse*, 'grant that I may be...' **sepulchro**: for *in sepulchro*.

907. **haud inscius**: 'fully conscious', a litotes.

908. **undanti in arma cruore**: 'as his blood spurted onto his armour'.

Appendix A

In English a line of verse is produced when words are arranged in a pattern formed by the natural stress or *ictus* of the words used. For example:

The ploúghman hómeward plóds his wéary wáy

has a pattern of unstressed syllable followed by stressed which is one of the commonest patterns in English verse. On the other hand if we write:

Hómeward plóds the ploúghman his wéary wáy

we do *not* have a line of verse since there is no regular pattern.

In early Latin verse also the pattern was formed by the natural stress of the words used. For example:

málum dábunt Metélli Náevio póetae

is a line of verse in the early Saturnian metre, and verse with stress patterns continued to flourish in less educated circles as is indicated by the following line of a military marching song:

écce Caésar núnc triúmphat qúi subégit Gálliás.

THE LATIN HEXAMETER

But a great change occured in Latin poetry when the Romans,

influenced by Greek verse and especially by Homer's *Iliad* and *Odyssey*, adopted the metre of the Greek hexameter and instead of a stress pattern based their verse on the *quantities of the syllables*. Often the quantity of a syllable coincides with the natural stress but this is by no means always the case.

Syllables in the Latin hexameter must contain either a vowel or a diphthong and are divided into two groups, those that are considered long/heavy (marked –) and those considered short/light (marked ᵕ). In general terms long syllables are considered to be twice the duration of short syllables. Furthermore a syllable containing a short vowel is considered to be long/heavy if the vowel is followed by two consonants though the vowel itself remains short. (For rules on the quantity of particular vowels see below.)

The hexameter consists of six metrical units called *feet*. The first four feet are either *dactyls* (– ∪ ∪) or *spondees* (– –), the fifth foot is nearly always a dactyl and the sixth is either a spondee or a *trochee* (– ∪). So the hexameter pattern looks like this:

1	2	3	4	5	6
– ∪ ∪	– ∪ ∪	– ∪ ∪	– ∪ ∪	– ∪ ∪	– –
– –	– –	– –	– –		– ∪

and a straightforward example is:

pāndĭtŭr|īntĕrĕā dŏmŭs|ōmnĭpŏtēntĭs Ŏlȳmpī.

In most lines a break or *caesura* occurs after the first syllable of either the third or fourth foot; in the line quoted above the caesura falls in the third foot between *interea* and *domus*. Other breaks may be used for particular effect. This caesura in the middle of the line, varying as it does between two different feet, helps to soften the relentless hexameter pattern and allows the poetry to flow more freely from one line into the next.

Elision is also frequent in Virgil's hexameters. This occurs when a word ending with a vowel or an 'm' is followed by a word beginning with a vowel or an '*h*'. In such cases the final syllable of the first word is lost, being slurred into the first syllable of the second word. For example *hasta est* becomes two syllables, *mensam ornat* becomes three and *magnum hostibus* becomes four.

SCANSION

To scan the following hexameter:

abnueram bello Italiam concurrere Teucris

1. Mark in any elision.

abnueram bello Italiam concurrere Teucris

2. Count back five syllables from the end and mark them dactyl and spondee or dactyl and trochee.

abnueram bello Italiam concurrere Teucris

3. Count the remaining syllables (10): this indicates that two dactyls and two spondees are required in the first four feet.

4. Mark any syllables you are sure are long.

abnueram bello Italiam concurrere Teucris

5. Complete the scansion to give two dactyls and two spondees and indicate the caesura (here in the fourth foot).

abnueram bello Italiam concurrere Teucris

The above mechanical way of scanning will always give the right answer but *it cannot be stressed too strongly* that the best way to appreciate the metre of Virgil, or of any other poet, is to read his verses, preferably aloud. Read them naturally, as if they were prose, and do not try to force some metrical pattern into them. If you pronounce words correctly, and omit or slur elided syllables, the rhythm of the verse will emerge of its own accord. There is no harm in learning the formal pattern or in scanning some lines with paper and pencil, but much more important is to *keep on reading the verses aloud* until you can hear their swing and rhythm at the first reading.

You will hear the thud of the Cyclopes' hammers in:

Illi inter sese magna vi bracchia tollunt

or the hoofs of a galloping horse in:

Quadrupedante putrem sonitu quatit ungula campum.

General notes:
(a) 'h' does not count as either a vowel or a consonant. It therefore cannot help to lengthen a syllable nor does it prevent elision.

E.g. *ămăt hōstēs* - 'at' not lengthened;

mūlti hŏstēs - 'i' is elided.

(b) The letter 'i' as well as being a vowel is sometimes a consonant, sounded like an English 'y' as in 'yet' for example. In such cases elision is avoided.

E.g. in *hāstām iēcĭt* there is no elision.

(c) The 'u' after 'q' is part of the consonant and not a separate vowel.

E.g. *nēquĕ* is two, *not* three syllables.

Some rules for deciding the quantity of a syllable are as follows:
1. A vowel followed by two consonants produces a long syllable.
    E.g. *defendit*; *amāt me*.

But if the two consonants are in the same word and the second is 'r', the vowel, if naturally short, may be short or long
    (e.g. *pătris*)
but if naturally long, it remains long
    (e.g. *ātra*).

2. 'x' and 'z' are double consonants.

3. All diphthongs are long.
   E.g. *rosāe*; *Clāudius*; *prōelia*.

4. If two vowels come together and do not form a diphthong, the first is usually short.
   E.g. *proelĭa*; *rosĕum*; *dĭes*.
   Exceptions are Greek words (where the Latin vowel represents a Greek diphthong) and the 'i' of *fio*.
   E.g. *Aenēas*; *fīam*.
   (Note however that in *fio* 'i' before 'er' is short. E.g. *fĭeri*).

5. Final 'i' is usually long.
   E.g. *dominī*; *audī*; *fortī*.
   But in *mihĭ*, *tibī̆*, *sibī̆*, *ubī̆*, *ibī̆* it is optional and in *nisĭ* it is short.

6. Final 'o' is usually long.
   E.g. *bellō*; *amō*; *rogabō*.
   But in *egŏ*, *duŏ*, *citŏ* and the adverb *modŏ* it is short.

7. Final 'u' is always long.
   E.g. *gradū*.

8. Final 'a' is short in nominative and vocative feminine singular of nouns and adjectives and in neuter plurals.
   E.g. *mensă* (nom.); *bellă*.
   Elsewhere it is long.
   E.g. *mensā* (abl.); *amā* (imperative).

9. Final 'e' is long in second conjugation singular imperative active, adverbs, fifth declension and pronouns.
   E.g. *monē*; *latē*; *dīē*; *mē*; *tē* ; *sē*.
   Elsewhere it is short.
   E.g. *tristĕ*; *regĕ*; *dominĕ*; *militĕ*.
   (See also the irregular adverb *bene*.)

Appendix B

IRREGULARITIES OF SCANSION IN AENEID X

1. Hiatus: elision not carried out.

(18) *o hominum*; (136) *buxo aut*; (141) *domo ubi*; (156) *duci Aeneia*.

2. Two vowels side by side treated as one sound.

(116) *aurēō*; (129) *Menesthēō*; (378) *dēest*; (402) *Rhoetēūs*; (487) *ēadem*; (496) *baltēī*; (704) *Nerēī*.

3. Abnormal lengthening.

(383) *dabāt hastam*; (394) *capūt Euandrius*; (433) *sinīt hinc*; (720) *profugūs hymenaeos*.

4. 'i' of 'semi' elided before a vowel.

(396) *sēm(i)ănĭmes*; (404) *sēm(i)ănĭmis*.

5. Older quantity retained.

(334) *stetĕrunt*.

6. Hypermetric *-que* elided before beginning of next line.

(781-2)...*caelum(que) aspicit*... (895-6) ...*Latini(que) advolat*...

Vocabulary

NOTE unusual meanings are followed by line reference(s).

ā, ab *prep. with abl.* from; by

abdūco -ere -duxi -ductum take away

abeo -īre -īvi *or* **-ii -itum** depart; get away (800)

abicio -ere iēci -iectum throw down

abnuo -ere -ui refuse; forbid

abscessus -ūs *m.* departure

absens -entis *adj.* absent, missing

absum abesse afui be absent, be away

ac *see* atque

accēdo -ere -cessi -cessum approach

accendo -ere -i -censum kindle; stir up

accipio -ere -cepi -ceptum receive; welcome; hear (675)

accurro -ere -curri -cursum run up; run towards

ācer -cris -cre *adj.* keen; energetic

acerbus -a -um *adj.* bitter

acervus -i *m.* heap, pile

acies -ēi *f.* army, battle-line; battle (543)

acūtus -a -um *adj.* sharp

ad *prep. with acc.* to, towards; at; near

adclīnis -e *adj.* leaning against

(with dat.)

addenseo -ēre close up, make compact

addo -ere addidi additum add

addūco -ere -duxi -ductum lead to

adeo -ire -ii -itum approach

adfīgo -ere -ixi -ixum attach to

adfor -āri -fātus speak to, address

adhuc *adv.* as yet

adicio -ere -iēci -iectum add, contribute

adigo -ere -ēgi -actum drive

adiuvo -āre -iūvi -iūtum help

adlābor -i -lapsus glide in; come to

adlacrimo -āre weep (at)

adloquor -i -locūtus address; appeal to

admoneo -ēre -ui -itum remind; urge on (587)

adnuo -ere -ui -ūtum nod assent

adoro -āre beseech

adsensus -ūs *m.* agreement

adsimulo -āre make like; imitate

adsisto -ere -stiti stand (by)

adsto -āre -stiti stand (by)

adsum -esse adfui be present; help *(with dat.)*

adsurgo -ere -surrexi -surrectum rise up

adulter -eri *m.* adulterer

86

adveho -ere -vexi -vectum carry, convey

advena -ae *c.* stranger

advenio -īre -vēni -ventum arrive, come to

adversus -a -um *adj.* facing; opposed

adverto, -ere -verti -versum turn (to)

advolo -āre fly to

aeger -gra -grum *adj.* sick, weak

aemulus -a -um *adj.* rivalling (*with dat.*)

aequālis -e *adj.* of the same age

aequo -āre make equal

aequor -oris *n.* sea; surface of sea; field of battle (451) (569); open space (444)

aequus -a -um *adj.* equal

aerātus -a -um *adj.* bronze-plated

aereus -a -um *adj.* made of bronze

aes aeris *n.* bronze; (*in pl.*) bronze weapons

aestas -ātis *f.* summer

aestuo -āre seethe

aestus -ūs *m.* tide; flood (292); current (687)

aetas -ātis *f.* age

aeternus -a -um *adj.* eternal, everlasting

aether -eris *m.* upper air; heaven

aetherius -a -um *adj.* heavenly

aevum -i *n.* age; life-span

age *imperat.* come now!

ager agri *m.* land

agger -eris *n.* rampart

agito -āre drive; disturb; (*trans.*) pass (*of time*)

agmen -inis *n.* army; rank (318); line of battle (769)

agnosco -ere -nōvi -nitum recognise

ago -ere ēgi actum drive, set in motion; do

agrestis -e *adj.* local, of the countryside

agricola -ae *m.* farmer

āio *defective verb* say

alacer -cris -cre *adj.* eager

albus -a -um *adj.* white

āles ālitis *c.* bird

aliēnus -a -um *adj.* not one's own; foreign

aliquis, aliquid someone, something; anyone, anything

aliter *adv.* otherwise

alius -a -ud *adj.* other, else

almus -a -um *adj.* kind; nourishing

altē *adv.* high; deeply

alter, altera, alterum *adj.* a second, another (*of two*)

altius *adv.* higher; deeper

altus -a -um *adj.* high; deep; noble (374) (737)

alvus -i *f.* belly

amārus -a -um *adj.* bitter

ambio -īre -īvi *or* **-ii -itum** go round, encircle

ambo -ae -o *adj.* both

āmens -entis *adj.* mad, distraught

amīcus -a -um *adj.* friendly

amnis -is *m.* river

amo -āre love

amor -ōris *m.* love; the god Love

amplector -i -exus embrace

an *conj.* or

an...an whether...or (681)

anceps -cipitis *adj.* balanced; uncertain

anhēlo -āre pant

anima -ae *f.* life; breath, blast

animus -i *m.* life; mind; heart;

courage

annōsus -a -um *adj*. aged, old

annus -i *m*. year

ante *adv*. before; sooner

ante *prep. with acc*. before; in front of (643)

antīquus -a -um *adj*. ancient

aper apri *m*. wild boar

aperio -īre -ui -ertum open

apex -icis *m*. helmet-crest, helmet

appāreo -ēre -ui -itum appear

apparo -āre prepare

applico -āre drive in

apto -āre fit, make ready

aqua -ae *f*. water

arātor -ōris *m*. ploughman

arbor -oris *f*. tree; oar (207)

arbusta -ōrum *n.pl*. bushes; trees

arcesso -ere -īvi -ītum summon

arcus -ūs *m*. bow

ardens -entis *adj*. blazing, afire; gleaming

ardeo -ēre arsi burn, blaze

ardor -ōris *m*. flame; heat

arduus -a -um *adj*. on high; steep; towering

argentum -i *n*. silver

arma -ōrum *n.pl*. arms; forces (150); battle (259)

armo -āre arm; man

armus -i *m*. shoulder

arrigo -ere -rexi -rectum raise, erect

arripio -ere -ripui -reptum seize, lay hold of

ars artis *f*. art, skill

arvum -i *n*. field, land, farmland; ground

arx arcis *f*. citadel, height; shelter (805)

aspecto -āre survey; look at

asper -era -erum *adj*. fierce; rough

aspicio -ere -spexi -spectum look, look at

ast *conj*. but

astū *adv*. deftly; cleverly

at *conj*. but

āter -ra -rum *adj*. dark, black; pitchy

atque *conj*. and; *after secus* than (272)

attingo -ere -tigi -tactum touch; reach (659)

attollo -ere raise, lift up

auctor -ōris *m*. author; cause; encourager (67)

audax -ācis *adj*. bold, daring

audens -entis *adj*. bold

audeo -ēre ausus dare

audio -īre -īvi *or* -ii -ītum hear

aufero -ferre abstuli ablatum take away, remove

augurium -i *n*. augury, omen

aura -ae *f*. air, breeze

aurātus -a -um *adj*. golden

aureus -a -um *adj*. golden

aurum -i *n*. gold

aut *conj*. or

aut...aut either...or

autem *conj*. but; now

auxilium -i *n*. aid, help; (*in pl*.) forces

avello -ere -vulsi -vulsum tear away

averto -ere -verti -versum turn away; carry off (78)

avītus -a -um *adj*. ancestral

avus -i *m*. ancestor; grandfather

bacchor -āri run riot

balteus -i *m*. belt

barba -ae *f*. beard

bellātor -ōris *m.* warrior; spirited (891)

bellum -i *n.* war

bipatens -entis *adj.* with double doors

biiugi -ōrum *m.pl.* two-horse chariot; pair of horses (595)

biiugus -a -um *adj.* twin-yoked

bonus -a -um *adj.* good

bracchium -i *n.* arm

brevis -e *adj.* shallow (289)

breviter *adv.* briefly

buxum -i *n.* box-wood

cado -ere cecidi casum fall

cadūcus -a -um *adj.* about to fall; doomed to fall (622)

caecus -a -um *adj.* unseen; blind; dark

caedes -is *f.* slaughter; dead people (245)

caedo -ere cecīdi caesum slay; beat; kick (404)

caelicola -ae *m. and f.* god

caelo -āre engrave, emboss

caelum -i *n.* sky, heaven; air (899)

caerulus -a -um *adj.* blue

calamus -i *m.* reed; arrow

calidus -a -um *adj.* hot

calx calcis *f.* heel; hoof (892)

campus -i *m.* level space; plain

caneo -ēre be grey, hoary

canis -is *c.* dog

cānities *acc.* -em, *abl.* -e white hair; hoariness; old age

cano -ere cecini cantum sing; foretell; sound, ring out (310)

cantus -ūs *m.* song

capillus -i *m.* hair

capio -ere cēpi captum take; arrive at (106)

caprea -ae *f.* wild goat

captīvus -a -um *adj.* captive, captured

captīvus -i *m.* prisoner

capulus -i *m.* hilt

caput -itis *n.* head, chief

carīna -ae *f.* keel

cārus -a -um *adj.* dear

castra -ōrum *n.pl.* camp

cāsus -ūs *m.* disaster; hazard; chance

caterva -ae *f.* troop, band

causa -ae *f.* cause, reason

cavus -a -um *adj.* hollow; convex (784)

cēdo -ere cessi cessum yield, give way; fail (276)

celero -āre hasten; accelerate

cēlo -āre hide

celsus -a -um *adj.* lofty

centēni -ae -a *adj.* a hundred each; a hundred

centum *indec.* a hundred

cerebrum -i *n.* brain

cerno -ere crēvi crētum see

cernuus -a -um *adj.* headforemost

certāmen -inis *n.* contest, struggle

certo -āre contend, fight, strive

certus -a -um *adj.* fixed, definite

cervix -īcis *f.* neck

cervus -i *m.* stag

ceu *conj.* just as; as if

chorēa -ae *f.* dance

chorus -i *m.* band, troop

cieo -ēre cīvi cītum call up, summon

cingo -ere cinxi cinctum surround, encircle

cinis -eris m. ashes

circulus -i *m.* circlet

circum *adv.* around

circumdo -āre surround
circumfero -ferre -tuli -lātum carry round
circumsto -āre -stiti surround
clāmo -āre shout
clāmor -ōris *m.* shout, cry
classis -is *f.* fleet, ships
claudo -ere clausi clausum close, shut; enclose
clāva -ae *f.* club, cudgel
clāvus -i *m.* tiller, helm
clipeus -i *m.* shield
coeo -īre -īvi *or* **-ii -itum** unite, come together
coeptum -i *n.* attempt
cōgo -ere coegi coactum compel
cohors cohortis *f.* band, company of soldiers
collum -i *n.* neck
coma -ae *f.* hair; mane
comes -itis *c.* friend, comrade
comētēs -ae *m.* comet
comito -āre *or* **comitor -āri** accompany
commercium -i *n.* traffic; trade
comminus *adv.* hand to hand
committo -ere -mīsi -missum entrust
cōmo -ere compsi comptum arrange, dress
compello -āre address
compōno -ere -posui -positum arrange, settle
concēdo -ere -cessi -cessum withdraw, depart; grant (906)
concha -ae *f.* seashell
concilio -āre win over
concilium -i *n.* council, meeting
conclāmo -āre shout together
concrēdo -ere -crēdidi -crēditum entrust

concurro -ere -curri clash, meet in battle (*with dat.*)
condo -ere -didi -ditum hide; bury; form
confero -ferre -tuli -latum engage in; (*with dat.*) engage in battle with
congredior -i -gressus meet with; join in battle
conicio -ere -iēci -iectum hurl; (*with se*) dive
cōnītor -nīti -nixus strain, struggle
coniungo -ere -iunxi -iunctum join; moor (653)
coniunx coniugis *m. and f.* husband; wife
conligo -ere -lēgi -lectum gather
conlūceo -ēre shine, gleam
cōnor -āri try
conscendo -ere -scendi -scensum board (a ship)
conscius -a -um *adj.* knowing; aware (*often with gen.*)
consīdo -ere -sedi sit, take seat; settle (780)
consisto -ere -stiti stand; make a stand
consors -tis *c.* partner, sharer (*with gen.*)
conspectus -ūs *m.* sight
conspicio -ere -spexi -spectum catch sight of
consuesco -ere -suēvi -suētum accustom oneself
consuētus -a -um *adj.* accustomed
consurgo -ere -surrexi -surrectum rise up
contendo -ere -di -tum hurl (521)
contiguus -a -um *adj.* within range (*with dat.*)
contineo -ēre -ui -tentum check,

restrain

contra *prep. with acc.* against

contra *adv.* in reply; in return; against; opposite

contristo -āre make gloomy, sadden

converto -ere -verti -versum change

convexum -i *n.* vault; arch (*of the sky*)

convexus -a -um *adj.* vaulted

coorior -īri -ortus arise

cor cordis *n.* heart; delight (252)

cornū -ūs *n.* horn; antler

corōna -ae *f.* crown; circle of defenders

corpus -oris *n.* body

corripio -ere -ripui -reptum take up, seize, seize on

corruo -ere -ui fall, sink

corusco -āre brandish (651)

costa -ae *f.* rib

crassus -a -um *adj.* thick

crastinus -a -um *adj.* of tomorrow

crēdo -ere -didi -ditum believe (*with dat.*); entrust (*with acc. and dat.*)

creo -āre beget; bear

crepīdo -inis *f.* ledge; quay

cresco -ere crēvi crētum increase; swell

crīmen -inis *n.* charge; guilt; crime

crīnis -is *m.* hair

crista -ae *f.* helmet-plume

crudēlis -e *adj.* cruel

crūdus -a -um *adj.* merciless, cruel

cruento -āre stain with blood

cruentus -a -um *adj.* bloody

cruor -ōris *m.* blood

culta -ōrum *n.pl.* cultivated land, farmland

cum *prep. with abl.* with, along with

cum *conj.* when

cunctor -āri -ātus halt; hesitate; turn slowly (717)

cunctus -a -um *adj.* all, whole

cupīdo -inis *f.* lust, desire

cupio -ere -īvi *or* **-ii -itum** desire

cūr *conj.* why?

cūra -ae *f.* care; object of care (132)

currus -ūs *m.* chariot; team of horses

cursus -ūs *m.* course

curvus -a -um *adj.* curving

cuspis -idis *f.* point; spear

de *prep. with abl.* from; down from; according to (832)

dea -ae *f.* goddess

dēbeo -ēre owe, ought

decet -ēre -uit it is proper

dēcīdo -ere -cīdi -cīsum cut off

decus decoris *n.* ornament; glory; pride

dēcutio -ere -cussi -cussum shake off

dēdecus -oris *n.* disgrace

dēdūco -ere -duxi -ductum derive (618)

dēfendo -ere -di -nsum defend; ward off; shelter (709)

dēfero -ferre -tuli -lātum carry down

dēflecto -ere -flexi -flexum deflect, turn aside

dēfodio -ere -fōdi -fossum bury

dēformo -āre defile; disfigure

dehisco -ere gape open

dēicio -ere -iēci -iectum hurl down; cut off (546)

dēiectus -a -um *adj.* downcast,

dismayed

deinde *adv.* then, thereupon

dēlābor -i -lapsus fall from, slip from

dēlūdo -ere -si -sum delude, deceive

dēmens -ntis *adj.* mad

dēmitto -ere -mīsi -missum send down

dēmoror -āri delay (*trans.*); keep waiting (30)

dēmum *adv.* at last

dēni -ae -a *adj.* ten at a time; ten

dens dentis *m.* tooth

densus -a -um *adj.* thick; close-locked

dēpendeo -ēre hang down

dēprehendo -ere -endi -ensum catch

dērigo -ere -rexi -rectum direct, aim

dēripio -ere -ui -eptum tear off; snatch away; pull out

dēsaevio -īre -ii rage furiously

dēsero -ere -ui -ertum desert, abandon

dēsilio -īre -ui -ultum jump down

dēsino -ere -ii -itum end, cease

dēsisto -ere -stiti -stitum cease from (*with dat.*)

dēspecto -āre look down on

dēsum -esse -fui be lacking

dētego -ere -texi -tectum uncover

dētono -āre -ui cease to thunder

dēturbo -āre dash down

deus -i *m.*: *gen.pl.* **deum** *or* **deōrum** god

dēvinco -ere -vīci -victum conquer; win (*a war*) (370)

dexter -era -erum *or* **-tra -trum** on the right

dextera -ae *or* **dextra -ae** *f.* the right hand

dicio -ōnis *f.* authority

dīco -ere dixi dictum speak; say; tell

dictum -i *n.* word

dies -ēi *m. or f.* day

diffugio -ere -fūgi scatter

diffundo -ere -fūdi -fūsum pour out

digitus -i *m.* finger

dignor -āri deign

dignus -a -um *adj. with abl.* worthy of; deserving of (668)

dīmitto -ere -mīsi -missum send away, remove

dīruo -ere -rui -rutum tear apart

dīrus -a -um *adj.* dread, dreadful

discedo -ere -cessi -cessum depart

discordia -ae *f.* dissension; mutiny

discors -cordis *adj.* discordant; opposed

discrepo -āre -ui differ

discrīmen -inis *n.* difference; distinction; division (382); dividing-line (511)

dispergo -ere -si -sum scatter, smash

dītissimus -a -um *adj.* richest

diū *adv.* for a long time

dīva -ae *f.* goddess

dīves dīvitis *adj.* rich

dīvido -ere -vīsi -vīsum part, divide

dīvīnus -a -um *adj.* divine

dīvus -i *m.*; *gen.pl.* **dīvum** god

do dare dedi datum give, grant

doceo -ēre -ui -tum teach

doctus -a -um *adj.* skilled, skilled in (*with gen.*)

dolor -ōris *m.* grief; bitterness; pain

dominus -i *m.* master
domus -ūs *f.* house; home; palace;
  temple
dōnec *conj.* until
dōno -āre give
dōnum -i *n.* gift
dorsum -i *n.* back; reef (303)
dūco -ere duxi ductum lead; derive
  (145); draw over (192); consider
  (669)
ductor -ōris *m.* leader
dūdum *adv.* a while ago, just now
dulcis -e *adj.* sweet; beloved (782)
dum *conj.* while; until
duo -ae -o two
duplex -icis *adj.* double; *in pl.* both
  (667)
dūrus -a -um *adj.* hard; tough;
  relentless
dux ducis *m.* guide; leader; master
  (574)

ē *or* **ex** *prep with abl.* from; instead
  of (221)
ebur eboris *n.* ivory
ecce *interjection* behold!
ēdīco -ere -dixi -dictum announce,
  proclaim
ēdo -ere -didi -ditum cause
ēdoceo -ēre -docui -doctum
  explain fully
ēdūco -ere -duxi -ductum pull out
  (744)
ēduco -āre rear
effero -ferre extuli ēlātum raise,
  lift
efferus -a -um *adj.* wild, fierce
effingo -ere -nxi -nctum fashion;
  imitate (640)
effor -fāri -fātus speak, utter
effundo -ere -fūdi -fūsum shed;

pour out; throw off (574, 893)
egēnus -a -um *adj.* needy
ego *pron.* I
ēgredior -i egressus disembark
ēgregius -a -um *adj.* outstanding;
  magnificent; noble (778)
ēicio -ere -iēci -iectum dislocate
  (894)
ēmētior -īri -mensus measure
ēmineo -ēre -minui project, stand
  out
ēminus *adv.* from a distance
ēmitto -ere -mīsi -missum throw
emo -ere ēmi emptum buy
enim *conj.* for
ensis -is *m.* sword
eo īre īvi *or* **ii itum** go, proceed
eques -itis *m.* cavalryman; rider;
  collectively cavalry
equidem *adv.* for my part; truly
equīnus -a -um *adj.* of a horse
equito -āre ride
equus -i *m.* horse
ergō *adv.* therefore
ēripio -ere -ui -reptum snatch,
  snatch away from
error -ōris *m.* mistake; wandering
ērumpo -ere -rūpi -ruptum burst
  out
et *conj.* and; also; even
et...et both...and
etiam *adv.* also; even
ēvādo -ere vāsi -vāsum escape
  from
ēventus -ūs *m.* event; outcome
ēverto -ere -verti -versum destroy;
  overthrow
ex *see* **ē**
exanimis -e *adj.* dead
excidium -i *n.* destruction,
  devastation; (*pl.*) ruins

excieo -īre -īvi *or* **-ii -itum** arouse
excipio -ere -cēpi -ceptum catch; receive
excutio -ere -cussi -cussum throw out; shake out; *in pass.* glance from (777)
exerceo -ēre -ui -itum work at: *trans.* keep busy (808)
exercitus -ūs *m.* army
exhaurio -īre -hausi -haustum exhaust; endure to the end
exigo -ere -ēgi -actum drive out; drive; finish; live out (53)
exiguus -a -um *adj.* small
exitium -i *n.* destruction; death (850)
exitus -ūs *m.* end
exorsa -ōrum *n.pl.* beginnings
expello -ere -puli -pulsum drive off, drive out
expendo -ere -di -sum pay
expers -tis *adj.* devoid of (*with gen.*)
expertus -a -um *adj.* experienced in (*with gen.*)
expōno -ere -posui -positum land *trans.*; cast out; put out (654)
expostus *for* **expositus -a -um** exposed to (*with dat.*)
expugno -āre take by storm; ravage
exseco -āre -secui -sectum cut out
exspīro -āre breathe one's last, die
exsulto -āre leap; dash up; prance
exsupero -āre overcome, surmount
extendo -ere -di -tum *or* **-sum** extend
externus -a -um *adj.* foreign
exterreo -ēre -ui -itum terrify
extrēmus -a -um *adj.* last; in the rear

exūro -ere -ussi -ustum burn out
exuviae -ārum *f.pl.* spoils

facies -ēi *f.* face; appearance
facio -ere fēci factum make; do; bring about (875)
factum -i *n.* deed
factus -a -um *adj.* wrought (*of gold*) (527)
fallo -ere fefelli falsum deceive, trick
falsus -a -um *adj.* false
fāma -ae *f.* fame; rumour (510) (679)
fames -is *f.* hunger
fātidicus -a -um *adj.* prophetic
fatīgo -āre tire
fātum -i *n.* fate, destiny
fax facis *f.* torch, fire-brand
femur -oris *or* **-inis** *n.* thigh
ferio -īre strike; make a treaty
fero ferre tuli lātum carry; bring; endure; *in pass.* rush, be carried along
ferox -ōcis *adj.* savage; high-spirited
ferreus -a -um *adj.* of iron
ferrum -i *n.* iron; sword; spear; knife
ferunt *from* **fero** they say (that) (189)
ferus -a -um *adj.* fierce, wild
fervidus -a -um *adj.* fiery, hot
fervor -ōris *m.* heat; fury
fibra -ae *f.* fibre; *in pl.* entrails
fides -ēi *f.* belief; loyalty
fīdo -ere fīsus sum trust (*with dat. or abl.*)
fidūcia -ae *f.* confidence, reliance
fīdus -a -um *adj.* faithful

fīgo -ere fixi fixum plant; fasten; make fast; pierce (343, 778)
figūra -ae *f.* shape
fīlius -i *m.* son
fīlum -i *n.* thread
findo -ere fidi fissum cleave
fīnis -is *m.* end; *in pl.* territory
fīo fieri factus sum be made; become; occur
flāmen -inis *n.* blast
flamma -ae *f.* flame
flavens -entis *adj.* golden, yellow
flaveo -ēre be golden, yellow
flecto -ere -xi -xum turn; wheel
fleo flēre flēvi flētum weep
fluctuo -āre waver
fluctus -ūs *m.* wave
fluito -āre float
flūmen -inis *n.* river
fluo -ere fluxi fluxum flow
fluxus -a -um *adj.* weak, unstable
foedē *adv.* foully
foedus -eris *n.* bargain, treaty
(for) fāri fātus speak; say
forma -ae *f.* shape, form
formīdo -inis *f.* terror, dread
fornix -icis *m.* arch, overhang
fors *abl.* **forte** *f.* chance
forte *adv.* by chance
fortasse *adv.* perhaps
fortis -e *adj.* brave
fortūna -ae *f.* luck; fortune; good fortune
fossa -ae *f.* ditch, moat
foveo -ēre fōvi fōtum foster; support (838)
fragmen -inis *n.* fragment, broken piece
frango -ere fregi fractum break
frāter fratris *m.* brother
fraus fraudis *f.* deceit; harm

fremo -ere fremui murmur; rustle; roar (572)
frēna -ōrum *n.pl.* reins
frequens -entis *adj.* in crowds
fretum -i *n.* sea *usually pl.*
frīgidus -a -um *adj.* cold
frons frondis *f.* leaf
frons frontis *f.* front; forehead
frustra *adv.* in vain
fuat *see note* line 108
fuga -ae *f.* flight, way of escape
fugax -ācis *adj.* fleeing, in flight
fugio -ere fūgi flee; fly; escape; *trans.* flee from
fugo -āre put to flight
fulgens -entis *adj.* shining, gleaming
fulgeo -ēre fulsi shine, gleam
fulmen -inis *n.* lightning, thunderbolt
fulvus -a -um *adj.* tawny; auburn-haired
fūmo -āre smoke
fundo -ere fūdi fūsum pour, pour out; spread (838)
fundus -i *m.* base, foundation
fūnis -is *m.* cable
fūnus -eris *n.* death
furiae -ārum *f.pl.* madness, frenzy, ravings
furo -ere rage
furor -ōris *m.* rage, furious anger
furtum -i *n.* theft; guile, treachery
fūsus -a -um *adj.: see* **fundo,** spread out; flowing

galea -ae *f.* helmet
gaudeo -ēre gavīsus rejoice
gaudium -i *n.* pleasure, delight
geminus -a -um *adj.* twin
gemitus -ūs *m.* groan

gemma -ae *f.* jewel
generōsus -a -um *adj.* high-born; *of places* rich in
genetrix -īcis *f.* mother
genitor -ōris *m.* father
gens gentis *f.* race, people; offspring (228)
genū -ūs *n.* knee
genus -eris *n.* race, lineage
germāna -ae *f.* sister
germānus -i *m.* brother
gigno -ere genui genitum produce; beget
gladius -i *m.* sword
glaucus -a -um *adj.* grey
globus -i *m.* mass
gloria -ae *f.* glory, fame
gnātus -i *m. same as* natus
gōrytus -i *m.* quiver
gradior -i gressus walk; stride (572)
grando -inis *f.* hail
grātus -a -um *adj.* welcome, pleasing; dear
gravidus -a -um *adj.* pregnant
gravis -e *adj.* serious; grievous; heavy; stately; grim
graviter *adv.* heavily
gravor -āri -ātus grudge (628)
gremium -i *n.* bosom
gressus -ūs *m.* step
grus gruis *c.* crane
gurges -itis *m.* water; sea
guttur -uris *n.* throat
gyrus -i *m.* circle

habēna -ae *f.* rein
habeo -ēre have; hold; keep (827)
hāc *adv.* by this way
hactenus *adv.* to this extent
haereo -ēre haesi haesum stick,

cling to (*with dat.*)
harundineus -a -um *adj.* of reeds
harundo -inis *f.* reed
hasta -ae *f.* spear
hastīle -is *n.* spear
haud *adv.* not
haurio -ire hausi haustum drain; drink in (648)
hērōs -ōis *m.* hero
heu *interjection* alas!
hīc haec hōc this
hīc *adv.* here; in this
hiems hiemis *f.* winter; storm
hinc *adv.* from here; after this; from him
hinc...hinc on one side...on the other
hio -are gape, open the mouth
hirsūtus -a -um *adj.* shaggy
hispidus -a -um *adj.* hairy
hodiē *adv.* today
homo -inis *m.* man
honestus -a -um *adj.* fine, lovely
honos -ōris *m.* honour
horrens -entis *adj.* bristling
horreo -ēre bristle; shudder at; fear (880)
horridus -a -um *adj.* ragged (408)
hortor -āri urge, encourage
hospitium -i *n.* hospitality
hostīlis -e *adj.* hostile; of the enemy
hostis -is *m. and f.* enemy
huc *adv.* to here, this way
hūmānus -a -um *adj.* human
humo -āre bury
humi on the ground, in the ground
humus -i *f.* ground
hymenaeus -i *m.* marriage

iaceo -ēre lie; lie dead (737)

iacio -ere iēci iactum throw, brandish

iacto -āre toss, throw about, fling

iaculum -i *n*. javelin

iam *adv*. now; already

iam...iam at one moment...at another

ictus -ūs *m*. blow; impact (484)

idcirco *adv*. on account of that; therefore

īdem eadem idem *adj*. same

ignārus -a -um *adj*. ignorant, unaware; a stranger (706)

ignipotens -entis *adj*. ruler of fire, *epithet of Vulcan*

ignis -is *m*. fire

ignōtus -a -um *adj*. unknown

īlia -ium *n.pl*. groin

ille illa illud that; he, she, it

illūc *adv*. to there, that way

imāgo -inis *f*. image; phantom (643)

immānis -e *adj*. enormous, huge

immineo -ēre threaten; overhang (*with dat*.)

immisceo -ēre -miscui -mixtum mix in; mingle with (664) (*with dat*.)

immitto -ere -mīsi -missum cast at; loosen (229); launch against

immolo -āre sacrifice; slay

immōtus -a -um *adj*. unmoved

impār -aris *adj*. unequal

impastus -a -um *adj*. hungry

impavidus -a -um *adj*. unafraid

impedio -īre hinder, hamper; entangle

impello -ere -pūli -pulsum drive, urge on

imperditus -a -um *adj*. not destroyed

imperium -i *n*. command; power; rule; empire

imperterritus -a -um *adj*. undismayed

impleo -ēre -ēvi -ētum fill

implico -āre pin down (894)

implōro -āre appeal to

impōno -ere -sui -situm place on

imprimo -ere -ssi -ssum engrave

improbus -a -um *adj*. remorseless

īmus -a -um *adj*. lowest; bottom of

in *prep*. *with acc*. into; against

in *prep*. *with abl*. in, at

inānis -e *adj*. empty; unsubstantial; useless (758)

incautus -a -um *adj*. reckless

incēdo -ere -cessi -cessum advance

incendium -i *n*. fire

incendo -ere -di -sum set ablaze

incesto -āre pollute, defile

incido -ere -di -cāsum fall on; hit (477)

incipio -ere -cēpi -ceptum begin

inclūdo -ere -clūsi -clūsum shut in; set in

incolumis -e *adj*. safe, unharmed

increpito -āre chide, rebuke

increpo -āre taunt, reprove

incumbo -ere -cubui -cubitum lie on; bend to; put weight on (*with dat*.)

inde *adv*. from there; then

indignus -a -um *adj*. monstrous; disgraceful

indiscrētus -a -um *adj*. indistinguishable

indoles -is *f*. nature, temperament

indulgeo -ēre -si -tum indulge

induo -ere -ui -ūtum put on; clothe; *see note* 682

inermus -a -um *or* **inermis -e** *adj.*
unarmed, unprotected

iners -ertis *adj.* idle; helpless (595)

inexhaustus -a -um *adj.*
inexhaustible

infandus -a -um *adj.* unspeakable

infectus -a -um *adj.* unwrought,
unfinished

infēlix -icis *adj.* unhappy; unlucky

infensus -a -um *adj.* hostile

inferiae -ārum *f.pl.* offerings to the
dead

infero -ferre -tuli -lātum bring in;
launch (364); *with se* go,
advance

infestus -a -um *adj.* hostile

infit *defective verb* begins (to
speak)

infligo -ere -flixi -flictum dash
against

infremo -ere -ui growl, roar

infrendens -entis *adj.* gnashing

infrēnis -e *adj.* unbridled

infringo -ere -ēgi -actum break

infula -ae *f.* fillet, band of wool

ingemo -ere -ui -itum lament,
groan

ingens -entis *adj.* huge; mighty

inglōrius -a -um *adj.* without glory

ingrātus -a -um *adj.* ungrateful
(for) (*with gen.*)

ingredior -i -gressus enter; walk
(767)

inguen -inis *n.* groin

inhaereo -ēre -haesi -sum cling to
(*with abl.*)

inhorreo -ēre -ui bristle

inicio -ere -iēci -iectum lay hands
on

inimīcus -a -um *adj.* hostile

inīquus -a -um *adj.* perverse;

hostile; uneven; unequal

inligo -āre impede; entangle

inno -āre swim in; sail along

innocuus -a -um *adj.* undamaged

inoffensus -a -um *adj.*
unobstructed; undisturbed

inquam, *3rd person* **inquit,** say

inreparābilis -e *adj.* irretrievable

inrigo -āre irrigate; water

inrīto -āre vex, annoy, provoke
(644)

inritus -a -um *adj.* empty; useless;
in vain

inruo -ere -ui rush at, charge

insānia -ae *f.* madness

inscius -a -um *adj.* not knowing,
unwitting

insidiae -ārum *f.pl.* ambush, snare

insīdo -ere -sēdi -sessum settle
upon

insigne -is *n.* badge; sign; emblem

insignis -e *adj.* conspicuous;
illustrious; renowned

insons -tis *adj.* innocent, guiltless

instauro -āre renew

insto -āre institi press hard on;
chase; (*with dat.*) *intrans.* press
hard

insuētus -a -um *adj.*
unaccustomed

insula -ae *f.* island

insulto -āre triumph, exult over

intactus -a -um *adj.* untouched,
unharmed

intempestus -a -um *adj.* unhealthy

intemptātus -a -um *adj.* untried

intepesco -ere -ui grow warm

inter *prep. with acc.* among;
between

intercipio -ere -cēpi -ceptum
intercept

interea *adv.* meanwhile
interimo -ere -ēmi -emptum kill
interpres -etis *c.* mediator
intexo -ere -ui -tum weave
intorqueo -ēre -torsi -tortum hurl
intra *prep. with acc.* within
inultus -a -um *adj.* unavenged
inundo -āre overflow
inūtilis -e *adj.* helpless (794)
invādo -ere -vāsi -vāsum attack
invenio -īre -vēni -ventum find
invictus -a -um *adj.* invincible
invidia -ae *f.* ill-will, unpopularity
invītus -a -um *adj.* unwilling
ipse ipsa ipsum himself, herself,
    itself; self
īra -ae *f.* anger
īrascor -i -ātus be angry; vent
    anger
is ea id he, she, it; that
iste ista istud that (*of yours*)
istīc *adv.* there
ita *adv.* so
iter itineris *n.* road, path, way
iterum *adv.* again; a second time
iuba -ae *f.* crest
iubeo -ēre iussi iussum order
iugālis -e *adj.* nuptial
iugulum -i *n.* throat
iugum -i *n.* yoke; team (594)
iungo -ere iunxi iunctum join
iurgium -i *n.* quarrel; abuse
iussum -i *n.* command
iustus -a -um *adj.* just, proper,
    right
iuvenis -is *m.* young man, youth
iuventūs -ūtis *f.* youth; young men
iuvo -āre iūvi iūtum help, assist;
    avail

labo -āre totter, waver

labor -ōris *m.* toil, trouble, labour
lābor -i lapsus fall, slip; drift (687)
lacertus -i *m.* upper arm
lacesso -ere -īvi *or* -ii -itum
    provoke, harass
lacrima -ae *f.* tear
lacteus -a -um *adj.* milk-white
laetor -āri rejoice
laetus -a -um *adj.* glad, happy
laeva -ae *f.* left hand
laevus -a -um *adj.* left; baneful
    (275)
lambo -ere -i lick
langueo -ēre fall back, sink
lānūgo -inis *f.* down
lapsus -ūs *m.* a fall
largior -īri -ītus grant, bestow
largus -a -um *adj.* liberal
lātē *adv.* far and wide
latebrae -ārum *f.pl.* hiding-place
lateo -ēre lie hidden
lātus -a -um *adj.* wide
latus -eris *n.* side, flank
laudo -āre praise
laus laudis *f.* praise; renown; *in pl.*
    noble deeds (825)
lavo -āre lavi wash, bathe
lectus -a -um *adj.* chosen
legio -ōnis *f.* force, army
lego -ere lēgi lectum choose, pick;
    gather up
leo -ōnis *m.* lion
lētifer -era -erum *adj.* deadly
lētum -i *n.* death
levis -e *adj.* light; insubstantial
    (663)
levo -āre relieve; free; rest (834)
liber -era -erum *adj.* free (from)
lībro -āre poise, brandish; balance
    (480)
licet -ēre licuit it is allowed

licitus -a -um *adj.* allowed, permitted
līmen -inis *n.* threshold
līmes -itis *m.* path
līneus -a -um *adj.* of linen
lingua -ae *f.* tongue; speech
linquo -ere līqui leave
liquidus -a -um *adj.* clear
lītus -oris *n.* beach, shore
loco -āre place; settle
locus -i *m.*: *pl.* **loca** *n.* place; ground; position
longē *adv.* long after; at a distance, from far away
longum *adv.* for a long time (740)
longus -a -um *adj.* long
loquor -i locūtus speak
lōrica -ae *f.* breastplate
lūceo -ēre luxi shine, glitter
luctus -ūs *m.* grief
lūdo -ere -si -sum mock
lūgubris -e *adj.* baneful
lūmen -inis *n.* light; eye (746)
lūo -ere lui pay for
lustro -āre move around
lux lūcis *f.* light; day; dawn
lympha -ae *f.* water

macto -āre kill
maculo -āre stain, dishonour
maereo -ēre grieve, be sorrowful
maestus -a -um *adj.* sad
mage *same as* magis
magis *adv.* more
magnanimus -a -um *adj.* heroic
magnus -a -um *adj.* great; loud (873)
māior -ius *adj.* greater
māla -ae *f.* cheek
mālo malle malui prefer
malum -i *n.* evil; setback

malus -a -um *adj.* wrong, evil
mandātum -i *n.* command
maneo -ēre mansi mansum remain; *trans.* await
mānes -ium *m.pl.* spirits of the dead
manus -ūs *f.* hand; force, band
mare -is *n.* sea
marmor -oris *n.* surface (*of the sea*)
māter mātris *f.* mother
mātūrus -a -um *adj.* ripe; full
maximus -a -um *adj.* greatest; tallest; mighty (685)
meditor -āri practise
medius -a -um *adj.* middle (of), in the middle
melior -ius *adj.* better
membrum -i *n.* limb
memor -oris *adj.* mindful
memorandus -a -um *adj.* famous
memoro -āre tell, relate; say (680)
mens mentis *f.* mind; senses (899)
mensa -ae *f.* table; hospitality (460, 516)
mentum -i *n.* chin
mereo -ēre -ui -itum deserve
mergo -ere -si -sum sink, plunge
mēta -ae *f.* goal
metallum -i *n.* metal; *in pl.* mine
meto -ere messui messum mow down
metuo -ere -ui -ūtum fear
metus -ūs *m.* fear
meus -a -um *adj.* my, mine
mico -āre -ui gleam; flicker; twitch (396)
mīlia -ium *n.pl.* thousands
mille *indecl.* one thousand
minae -ārum *f.pl.* threats
minax -ācis *adj.* threatening

ministro -āre attend to (218) (*with dat.*)

minor -āri threaten (*with dat.*)

minor -ōris *adj.* smaller, lesser

minus *adv.* less

mirābilis -e *adj.* wonderful

mīror -āri -ātus wonder at

mīrus -a -um *adj.* strange, wonderful

misceo -ēre miscui mixtum mix; involve in; cause confusion in (721)

miser -era -erum *adj.* wretched, unhappy

miserandus -a -um *adj.* pitiable

misereor -ēri -itus pity (*with gen.*)

miseresco -ere have pity on (*with gen.*)

miseror -āri pity; bewail

missile -is *n.* dart, missile

missilis -e *adj.* to be hurled

mitto -ere mīsi missum send; throw, hurl

modus -i *m.* way, method; moderation (502)

moenia -ium *n.pl.* walls, fortifications

moerus *same as* **mūrus**

mōles -is *f.* mass; bulk (771)

mōlior -īri hurl (131); force (477)

mollis -e *adj.* soft; pliant

moneo -ēre advise; warn

monita -ōrum *n.pl.* prophecies, warnings

monitus -ūs *m.* warning, prophecy

mons montis *m.* mountain

monstrum -i *n.* marvel (637)

mora -ae *f.* delay; hindrance; barrier (485)

morbus -i *m.* disease

moribundus -a -um *adj.* dying

morior -i mortuus die

moror -āri -ātus delay

mors mortis *f.* death

morsus -ūs *m.* bite

mortālis -e *adj.* mortal; of men

mortālis -is *c.* man; human being

mōs mōris *m.* way; manner; custom

moveo -ēre mōvi motum move, rouse, stir up; turn over (890)

mox *adv.* soon

mūcro -ōnis *m.* sword-point

multum *adv.* much; often (839)

multus -a -um *adj.* much; *pl.* many

murmur -uris *n.* murmur

murmuro -āre murmur

mūrus -i *m.* wall

mūto -āre change

mūtuus -a -um *adj.* mutual; on both sides (755)

nam, namque *conj.* for

nascens -entis *adj.* new-born

nascor -i nātus be born; rise

nātūra -ae *f.* nature

nātus -i *m.* son

nauta -ae *m.* sailor

nāvis -is *f.* ship

nē *particle of negative command* do not...

nē *conj.* lest

-ne *questioning particle*

nebula -ae *f.* mist

nec *or* **neque** *adv.* nor

nec...nec: neque...neque neither... nor

nefandus -a -um *adj.* monstrous; abominable

nefas *n. indecl.* sin, crime

nego -āre deny

neo -ēre nēvi embroider

nepos -ōtis *m.* grandson; descendant

neque *conj. same as* nec

nēquīquam *adv.* in vain; helplessly

nervus -i *m.* sinew; bowstring

nescius -a -um *adj.* ignorant (of) (*with gen.*)

neu *or* **nēve** *conj.* and lest; and that not

ni *conj.* if...not; unless

nihil *n. indecl.* nothing; in no way; nor

nil *n. indecl.* in no way

nimbus -i *m.* cloud

nītor -i -sus *or* **-xus** press on (*with abl.*)

no -āre swim

noctivagus -a -um *adj.* night-wandering

nōdus -i *m.* knot

nōmen -inis *n.* name

nōn *adv.* not

nōnne *interrog. particle* is not?

nōs *pron.* we

noster nostra nostrum *adj.* our, of us; my

nōtus -i *m.* south wind

notus -a -um *adj.* known

noverca -ae *f.* stepmother

novus -a -um *adj.* new, fresh; strange

nox noctis *f.* night

nūbes -is *f.* cloud

nūbila -ōrum *n.pl.* clouds

nullus -a -um *adj.* no; not any

num *in indirect question* whether

num *interrog. particle* surely...not?

nūmen -inis *n.* divine power, god

numerus -i *m.* number

nunc *adv.* now

nunquam *adv.* never

nusquam *adv.* nowhere

nūtus -ūs *m.* nod

nympha -ae *f.* nymph

ō *with voc. in addresses*

ob *prep. with acc.* because of

obdūco -ere -duxi -ductum cover up

obeo -īre -īvi *or* **-ii -itum** face; survey (447); cover (483); *with mortem* die

ōbex -icis *f.* bar, barrier

obicio -ere -iēci -iectum throw in the way of (*with acc. and dat.*)

oblīviscor -i -lītus forget (*usually with gen.*)

obnītor -i -sus *or* **-xus** strive, strain

obnixus -a -um *adj.* steadfast; not giving way

oborior -īri -ortus rise

obruo -ere -ui -utum overwhelm

obsideo -ēre -sēdi -sessum besiege; hem in (120)

obsidio -ōnis *f.* siege, blockade

obsto -āre -stiti oppose (*with dat.*)

obtendo -ere -tendi -tentum spread in front of

obtestor -āri implore

obtrunco -āre slay

obvius -a -um *adj.* in the way; to meet (552, 877); facing (*with dat.*) (694)

obvius īre to meet (*with dat.*)

occido -ere -cidi -cāsum fall; perish

occīdo -ere -cīdi -cīsum kill

occubo -āre lie; rest (*in the grave*)

occumbo -ere -cubui -cubitum fall down

occupo -āre forestall; attack first (699)

occurro -ere -curri -cursum run to meet (*with dat.*)

ōcior -ius *comparative adj.* swifter;
swiftly (786)
oculus -i *m.* eye
ōdi ōdisse hate
odium -i *n.* hatred
offero -ferre obtuli offer; *with se*
go towards
olim *adv.* formerly; in the future
olli *for* illi *dat. sing. of* ille
olōrīnus -a -um *adj.* of a swan
ōmen -inis *n.* omen
omnipotens -entis *adj.* all-
powerful
omnis -e *adj.* all, every
onero -āre load; pile
onus oneris *n.* weight
opācus -a -um *adj.* dark
opes *f.pl.* resources; forces
opīmus -a -um *adj.* rich
opperior -īri -pertus await
oppōno -ere -posui -positum put
opposite; oppose
optātum -i *n.* a wish
optimus -a -um *adj.* best;
excellent; loving (557)
opto -āre wish, wish for, desire
opus operis *n.* work, job; deed
(792)
ōra -ae *f.* shore; district; rim (243)
orbis -is *m.* circle
orīgo -inis *f.* origin; lineage (618)
orno -āre adorn; equip
ornus -i *f.* ash tree
ōro -āre beg, beg for; speak
orsa -ōrum *n.pl.* beginnings;
intentions (632)
ōs ōris *n.* mouth; face
os ossis *n.* bone
ostrum -i *n.* purple
ovo *defective verb* exult, triumph

paciscor -i pactus agree, covenant
pactus -a -um *adj.* betrothed
paean -ānis *m.* shout of triumph
palleo -ēre -ui be pale
pallidus -a -um *adj.* pale
palma -ae *f.* palm; hand (596)
pālor -āri wander; straggle
palus -ūdis *f.* marsh
pando -ere pandi throw open,
open wide
(pango -ere) pepigi pactum make
a compact
pār paris *adj.* equal; similar (568,
742)
parco -ere peperci parsum spare
(*with dat.*); have regard for
(880)
parens -entis *c.* parent; father;
mother; (*pl.*) ancestors
pāreo -ēre -ui obey (*with dat.*)
pariter *adv.* equally; together
(865)
parma -ae *f.* shield
paro -āre prepare
pars partis *f.* part; side; direction
partim *adv.* partly, in part
parvus -a -um *adj.* small, little;
young
pasco -ere pāvi pastum feed
pastor -ōris *m.* shepherd
pater patris *m.* father
paternus -a -um *adj.* of a father;
paternal
patiens -entis *adj.* able to bear
(*with gen.*)
patior -i passus suffer, endure;
allow
patria -ae *f.* fatherland, country
patrius -a -um *adj.* ancestral,
father's
pauci -ae -a *adj.* few

pax pācis *f.* peace: approval (31)
peccātum -i *n.* sin
pectus -oris *n.* breast, heart
pecus -udis *f.* animal; cattle
pedes peditis *adj.* on foot
pedester -tris -tre *adj.* on foot
pelagus -i *n.* sea; open sea
pellis -is *f.* hide
pello -ere pepuli pulsum drive away
pendeo -ēre pependi hang *intrans.*; bend (586)
penetrābilis -e *adj.* piercing, penetrating
penitus *adv.* deep within
per *prep. with acc.* through, over, by means of (290); *in oaths or entreaties* by, in the name of
peragro -āre travel through, wander among
perdo -ere -didi -ditum destroy
pereo -īre -īvi *or* **-ii -itum** perish
perfero -ferre -tuli -lātum endure; bear to the end
perfidus -a -um *adj.* treacherous
perforo -āre pierce
perfringo -ere -frēgi -fractum break through
perfundo -ere -fūdi -fūsum drench; bathe
perīculum *or* **perīclum -i** *n.* danger
perimo -ere -ēmi -emptum kill, slay
permisceo -ēre -miscui -mixtum mix, mingle
persequor -i -secūtus follow, pursue
perstringo -ere -strinxi -strictum graze
perterreo -ēre -ui -itum dismay; terrify

pervenio -īre -vēni -ventum arrive; come to
pēs pedis *m.* foot
pestis -is *f.* curse; bane
peto -ere -īvi *or* **-ii -itum** make for; seek
pietas -ātis *f.* loyalty; love (812, 824)
pinguis -e *adj.* rich; fertile
pīnifer -fera -ferum *adj.* pine-clad
pinna -ae *f.* feather; plume
pīnus -i *or* **-ūs** *f.* pine; ship
piscis -is *m.* fish
pistris -is *f.*: *acc.* **-im** sea-monster
pius -a -um *adj.* dutiful; good; sinless (617)
pix pīcis *f.* pitch
placeo -ēre please (*with dat.*)
placet it pleases; is resolved
placidus -a -um *adj.* quiet, calm
placitus -a -um *adj.* resolved; pleased
plāga -ae *f.* blow, stroke
plūma -ae *f.* feather
pluit *impersonal* it rains
plūres -a *adj.* more
plūs *adv.* more
poena -ae *f.* penalty, punishment
pondus -eris *n.* weight
pōne *adv.* behind
pōno -ere posui positum put, place; lay down; ordain (623); abate (103)
pons pontis *m.* bridge; gangway
pontus -i *m.* sea, ocean
poples -itis *m.* knee
pōpuleus -a -um *adj.* of the poplar
populus -i *m.* people
porta -ae *f.* gate
porto -āre bring
posco -ere poposci demand;

challenge (661)

possum posse potui am able, can

post *prep. with acc.* after

postquam *conj.* after; when

potentia -ae *f.* power

potestas -ātis *f.* power; ruler

potior -īri -ītus get possession of (*with gen. or abl.*)

potius *adv.* rather

praebeo -ēre offer; provide

praeceps -cipitis *adj.* headlong

praecipio -ere -cēpi -ceptum seize first

praecipito -āre rush down

praeclārus -a -um *adj.* famous

praecordia -ōrum *n.pl.* heart

praeda -ae *f.* plunder

praedo -ōnis *m.* robber

praedūrus -a -um *adj.* very strong

praefero -ferre -tuli -lātum show, display

praefīgo -ere -fixi -fixtum fasten in front; point with

praegnans -antis *adj.* pregnant

praesāgus -a -um *adj.* foretelling; foreboding (*with gen.*)

praesens -entis *adj.* present

praeter *adv.* past

praeterea *adv.* moreover, besides

prātum -i *n.* field, meadow

precem *no nom. or gen. sing. f.* prayer, entreaty

preces -um *f.pl.* prayers

precor -āri pray, entreat

premo -ere pressi pressum press; oppress; drive; crush (54); suppress (465)

prīmaevus -a -um *adj.* youthful

prīmum *adv.* first

prīmus -a -um *adj.* first

princeps -ipis *adj.* first; leading; *as*

a noun leader

principium -i *n.* beginning

prior -us *adj.* first; earlier

pristinus -a -um *adj.* former, earlier

pristis -is *f.* sea monster

prius *adv.* before, previously; first (882)

pro *prep. with abl.* in front of; in return for; instead of

prōcēdo -ere -cessi -cessum advance

proceres -um *m.pl.* chieftains

procul *adv.* afar; from a distance; hard by (777, 835)

prōdeo -īre -īvi *or* **-ii -itum** run out; run forward

prōdo -ere -didi -ditum betray; give warning of (99)

proelium -i *n.* battle

profugus -i *m.* exile; fugitive

prōgenies -ēi *f.* offspring

prōicio -ere -iēci -iectum throw forward

prōles -is *f.* offspring; son

prōmitto -ere -mīsi -missum promise

prōmoveo -ēre -mōvi -mōtum move forward

prōnus -a -um *adj.* bending forward

prōpexus -a -um *adj.* hanging down

propinquo -āre approach; bring nearer (254)

propius *adv.* nearer

prōra -ae *f.* bow; ship

prōrumpo -ere -rūpi -ruptum burst forth; dash forward (796)

prospecto -āre look forward to; expect

prōtego -ere -xi -ctum protect; cover

prōtinus *adv.* at once, forthwith

prōturbo -āre drive away

prōvolvo -ere -volvi -volutum roll forward

proximus -a -um *adj.* nearest

pudor -ōris *m.* shame

puer pueri *m.* boy

pugna -ae *f.* battle

pulcher -chra -chrum *adj.* handsome

pulmo -ōnis *m.* lung

pulso -āre trample

pulvis -eris *m.* dust

puppis -is *f.*: *acc.* -im stern; ship

purpureus -a -um *adj.* purple

puto -āre think; consider

quā *adv.* where; by any way

quadriiugis -e *adj.* in a team of four

quadrupēs -pedis *adj.* four-footed; horse (892)

quaero -ere -sīvi *or* -sii -situm seek, search for; ask about

quālis -e *adj.* such as, like

quam *with adj.* as (763)

quamquam *conj.* although

quando *adv.* at any time (803)

quandoquidem *conj.* since

quantus -a -um *adj.* how great; how much

quartus -a -um *adj.* fourth

quaterni -ae -a *adj.* four each

quatio -ere shake

quattuor *indecl.* four

-que and

-que...-que both...and

queo quīre quīvi be able

quercus -ūs *f.* oak tree

querela -ae *f.* complaint

qui qua quod *indefinite adj.* any

qui quae quod *interrog. adj.* what? which?

qui quae quod *relative pron.* who; which

quianam *interrog.* why?

quicumque quaecumque quodcumque whoever, whatever

quid *interrog.* why?

quidem *adv.* indeed

quies -ētis *f.* rest, repose

quiesco -ere -ēvi -ētum rest; lie unused (836)

quiētus -a -um *adj.* quiet, peaceful

quīn *conj.* in fact (570); but that (615)

quingenti -ae -a *adj.* five hundred

quinquāginta *indec.* fifty

quinque *indec.* five

quis quid *interrog. pron.* who? what?

quīs *for* quibus

quis qua quid *indefinite pron.* anyone, anything

quisquam quaequam quidquam *or* quicquam anyone, anything

quisque quaeque quidque *or* quodque each

quisquis quodquod *or* quicquid whoever, whatever

quo *adv.* where to; where (60)

quod *conj.* because; but (631)

quondam *adv.* once, formerly

quoque *adv.* also

quot as many as

rāmus -i *m.* branch

rapidus -a -um *adj.* speedy, swift

rapio -ere -ui -tum snatch, seize;

plunder; *trans.* hurry along (178, 308, 574, 660)

rārus -a -um *adj.* thin

ratis -is *f.* ship

ratus -a -um *adj.* sure

recepto -āre draw back; recover

recidīvus -a -um *adj.* rebuilt

recipio -ere -cēpi -ceptum recover

reclūdo -ere -clūsi -clūsum open

recondo -ere -didi -ditum thrust; bury (816)

recursus -ūs *m.* retreat; ebbing

recūso -āre refuse; shrink from

reddo -ere -idi -itum give back, restore; reply

redeo -īre -īvi *or* **-ii -itum** return

redimio -īre -īvi *or* **-ii -itum** wreathe, bind

reditus -ūs *m.* return

redūco -ere -duxi -ductum bring back; draw back

refero -ferre rettuli relātum bring back; recall; reply

reficio -ere -fēci -fectum restore

reflecto -ere -xi -xum bend back; change (632)

rēgīna -ae *f.* queen

regio -ōnis *f.* region

rēgius -a -um *adj.* royal

regnātor -ōris *m.* ruler

regno -āre rule, have royal power

rego -ere rexi rectum guide, control

reicio -ere -iēci -iectum turn away

relābor -i -lapsus flow back

relinquo -ere -līqui -lictum leave

reminiscor -i remember

remitto -ere -mīsi -missum send back

remurmuro -āre murmur back

rēmus -i *m.* oar

reor rēri ratus think

repente *adv.* suddenly

repeto -ere -īvi *or* **-ii -itum** recall; mention again

reposco -ere claim

reprimo -ere -pressi -pressum hold back

rēs rēi *f.* thing; property

rēs rērum *f.pl.* universal affairs

respicio -ere -spexi -spectum look back at, look back

responsum -i *n.* reply, answer

resto -āre -stiti remain; be in store

resulto -āre rebound

rēte -is *n.* net

retineo -ēre -tinui -tentum hold back

retracto -āre clutch again

retraho -ere -traxi -tractum pull back

retro *adv.* back; backwards (573)

revoco -āre call back, recall

revolvo -ere -volvi -volūtum retrace; roll back; ebb (660)

rex rēgis *m.* king

rigidus -a -um *adj.* stiff

rīpa -ae *f.* river-bank

rīte *adv.* fittingly, correctly; happily

rōbur -oris *n.* spear (479)

rogito -āre keep asking

rogus -i *m.* funeral pyre

rostrum -i *n.* beak; prow

rota -ae *f.* wheel: *in pl.* chariot

roto -āre roll; swirl around; swing (577)

rubeo -ēre glow; be red

rudens -entis *m.* sheet, rope

rumpo -ere rūpi ruptum break, shatter

ruo -ere rui rush along, hasten; fall (338, 756)

rūpes -is *f.* rock; cliff

sacer -cra -crum *adj.* holy, sacred
sacerdōs -ōtis *c.* priest, priestess
sacro -āre dedicate
saepe *adv.* often
saevio -īre -ii -ītum rage; be fierce
saevus -a -um *adj.* fierce; cruel
sagitta -ae *f.* arrow
sāl salis *m.* salt; brine; sea
salio -īre -ui -tum leap
saltus -ūs *m.* a leap
salus -ūtis *f.* safety
sānē *adv.* by all means
sanguineus -a -um *adj.* blood-red
sanguis -inis *m.* blood
satis *adv.* enough
satius *adv.* better
saxum -i *n.* rock, boulder; cliff
scāla -ae *f. usually pl.* ladder
sceptrum -i *n.* sceptre
scindo -ere scidi scissum cut,
 cleave
scio -īre -īvi *or* -ii -itum know
scūtum -i *n.* shield
sē *pron.* himself, herself, itself,
 themselves
seco -āre secui sectum cut; cleave
 through; mark out (107)
secundus -a -um *adj.* favourable;
 exultant (266)
sēcūrus -a -um *adj.* careless (of);
 untroubled by (*with gen.*)
secus *adv.* otherwise
sed *conj.* but
sedeo -ēre sēdi sessum sit; settle
 down; stay fixed (785)
sēdes -is *f.* home
segnis -e *adj.* tardy, slow; cowardly
 (592)
semel *adv.* once

sēmianimis -e *or* sēmianimus -a
 -um *adj.* half-dead
sēmifer -era -erum *adj.* half-beast
(sēminex) sēminecis *adj.*
 half-dead
semper *adv.* always
senecta -ae *f.* old age
senior -ōris *adj.* older
senior -ōris *m.* old man
sensus -ūs *m.* sense
sententia -ae *f.* opinion; decision
sentio -īre sensi sensum feel;
 understand; realise
septem *indecl.* seven
septēni -ae -a *adj.* one from each
 of seven
sepulchrum -i *n.* tomb
sequax -ācis *adj.* following,
 pursuing
sequor -i secūtus follow; pay heed
 to (258)
sero -ere sēvi satum beget
sērus -a -um *adj.* late
servo -āre keep; save; watch for
 (288); observe
sescenti -ae -a *adj.* six hundred
sēsē *same as* se
seu...seu *or* sive...sive whether...or
sī *conj.* if
sīc *adv.* thus
sicco -āre dry; staunch
siccus -a -um *adj.* dry
sīdereus -a -um *adj.* starry
sīdus -eris *n.* star
signum -i *n.* signal
silentium -i *n.* silence
sileo -ēre be silent; *trans.* be silent
 about
silesco -ere become silent
silva -ae *f.* wood, forest
silvicola -ae *c.* living in woods

similis -e *adj.* alike, similar
simul *adv.* at the same time
sīn *conj.* but if
sine *prep. with abl.* without
sinister -ra -rum *adj.* on the left; wrong; unfavourable
sinistra -ae *f.* left hand
sino -ere sīvi situm *trans.* allow; *intrans.* let be
sinus -ūs *m.* fold; bosom
siquā *adv.* if in any way
sisto -ere stiti statum place, station; plant
sitis -is *f.* thirst; drought
sīve *see* seu
socer soceri *m.* father-in-law
socius -i *m.* ally, friend
sodālis -is *c.* comrade
sōl sōlis *m.* sun
sōlāmen -inis *n.* comfort, consolation
solium -i *n.* throne
sollicito -āre disturb; taunt (612)
sōlor -āri console; relieve
solum -i *n.* soil; foundation; ground
sōlus -a -um *adj.* alone; only
solvo -ere solvi solūtum loosen; break; absolve
somnium -i *n.* dream
somnus -i *m.* sleep
sonitus -ūs *m.* sound, noise
sons sontis *adj.* guilty
sonus -i *m.* sound
sōpio -īre -īvi *or* **-ii -itum** lull to sleep
soror -ōris *f.* sister
sors sortis *f.* part; lot, destiny
spatium -i *n.* course; distance; extent
spectātor -oris *c.* spectator

specto -āre look at; watch
specula -ae *f.* look-out place
speculor -āri examine; observe; espy
spēro -āre hope, hope for
spēs speī *f.* hope; ambition (371)
spīculum -i *n.* dart
spīna -ae *f.* spine
spīro -āre surge; heave
spolium -i *n.* spoil, booty
spūmeus -a -um *adj.* foaming
spūmo -āre foam
squāleo -ēre be stiff
stabulum -i *n.* stall, pen
stagnum -i *n.* pool
statio -ōnis *f.* anchorage
sterno -ere strāvi strātum lay low, strike down
stīpo -āre crowd together, mass
stirps stirpis *f.* stock, breed
sto stāre steti statum stand; be fixed; cost (*with dat. and abl.*)
strepo -ere -ui -itum make a clatter
strīdeo -ēre *or* **-ere -idi** whistle, whizz
stringo -ere strinxi strictum draw; graze
stupeo -ēre be amazed; gaze in amazement
suādeo -ēre suāsi suāsum advise, urge, persuade
sub *prep. with abl. and acc.* under; under cover of
subdūco -ere -duxi -ductum take away by stealth; steal away (*with acc. and abl.*)
subeo -īre -īvi *or* **-ii -itum** go under; approach (877); rise; advance (371); come to help (338); come into (824)

subigo -ere -ēgi -actum compel
subito *adv.* suddenly
subiungo -ere -iunxi -iunctum fix
beneath
sublevo -āre lift, raise
sublīmis -e *adj.* on high
subnecto -ere -nexui -nexum bind
up
subrēmigo -āre row beneath
subrīdeo -ēre -rīsi -rīsum smile
subsidium -i *n.* help, support
subsisto -ere -stiti -stitum halt
succēdo -ere -cessi -cessum come
to next; take the place of; enter
(*with dat.*)
succīdo -ere -cidi -cisum cut
through
succingo -ere -nxi -nctum gird;
surround
succurro -ere -curri -cursum help,
rescue
suggero -ere -gessi -gestum bring
up; collect
sulco -āre plough; cleave
sulcus -i *m.* furrow
sum esse fui be: *imperat.* esto so be
it
summa -ae *f.* chief command
summissus -a -um *adj.* humble
summus -a -um *adj.* highest;
supreme
super *adv.* besides; above; further
(42)
super *prep. with abl. and acc.* over;
about; on
superbus -a -um *adj.* proud,
haughty
superēmineo -ēre rise above,
overtop
superi -ōrum *c.pl.* gods; world
above (40)

supersto -āre stand over
supersum -esse -fui survive
superus -a -um *adj.* upper
supervolo -āre fly over
supplex -icis *adj.* suppliant
suprēmus -a -um *adj.* highest;
greatest; last
surgo -ere surrexi surrectum rise,
arise; grow (524)
suscito -āre rouse
suspicio -ere -spexi -spectum look
up at
sustento -āre hold up, support
sustineo -ēre -ui -tentum check;
withstand
sūta -ōrum *n.pl.* coat of mail
suus -a -um *adj.* his/her/its/their
own

tacitus -a -um *adj.* silent
taedet -ēre -uit it wearies
taeter -tra -trum *adj.* foul
talentum -i *n.* talent
tālis -e *adj.* such
tam *adv.* so
tamen *adv.* however
tandem *adv.* at last
tantum *adv.* so much
tantum -i *n.* so much (of)
tantus -a -um *adj.* so great
tardo -āre make slow; *intrans.* fail
(857)
taurus -i *m.* bull; bull's hide (785)
tectum -i *n.* hall; dwelling; roof
tegmen -inis *n.* covering; guard;
shield (887)
tego -ere texi tectum cover,
protect; bury (904)
tellus -ūris *f.* earth; land; ground
tēlum -i *n.* weapon
temno -ere tempsi temptum

despise

tempestas -ātis *f.* storm

tempto -āre try; excite; disturb

tempus -oris *n.* time; *pl.* temples (*of the head*) (538, 891)

tendo -ere tetendi tensum stretch out; strive, strain; (*with* in) make for

teneo -ēre tenui tentum hold; *intrans.* hold its course

tenor -ōris *m.* course

tenuis -e *adj.* thin; fine

tenus *prep. with gen. or abl.* down to; as far as

tepeo -ēre -ui be warm

ter *adv.* three times

terebinthus -i *f.* terebinth tree; turpentine tree

tergum -i *n.* back; layer (784); shield (718)

terra -ae *f.* land; country; earth

terreo -ēre frighten

tertius -a -um *adj.* third

thalamus -i *m.* bedroom; marriage bed

thōrax -ācis *m.* breastplate

tigris -idis *and* **-is** *c.* tiger

timeo -ēre fear

tollo -ere sustuli sublātum raise; lift; remove; rouse up (357)

tonsa -ae *f.* oar

torqueo -ēre torsi tortum hurl

torrens -entis *adj.* scorching hot; boiling

torrens -entis *m.* torrent

torvus -a -um *adj.* grim

tot *indecl.* so many

totidem *indecl.* just as many; the same number

totiens *adv.* so often

tōtus -a -um *adj.* whole (of)

traho -ere traxi tractum drag; prolong (888)

traicio -ere -iēci -iectum pierce

trano -āre swim across; fly across (265)

transeo -īre -ii -itum overlook; pass through (785)

transilio -īre -īvi *or* **-ui** leap over

transtrum -i *n.* bench; thwart

transverbero -āre pierce through

trecenti -ae -a *adj.* three hundred

tremefacio -ere -fēci -factum cause to tremble, shake

tremibundus -a -um *adj.* quivering

trepido -āre be afraid

trepidus -a -um *adj.* anxious; uncertain; fearful

trēs tria *adj.* three

triplex -icis *adj.* threefold, triple

trīs *same as* tres *in acc. pl.*

tristis -e *adj.* sad; grim (612)

tropaeum -i *n.* trophy

truncus -i *m.* trunk

trux trucis *adj.* grim; savage

tū *pron.* you *sing.*

tueor -ēri tuitus behold

tum *adv.* then

tumidus -a -um *adj.* swollen; puffed up, proud

tumulus -i *m.* grave

tunc *adv.* then

tundo -ere tutudi tunsum *or* **tūsum** strike

tunica -ae *f.* shirt

turba -ae *f.* crowd

turbidus -a -um *adj.* confused; wild

turbo -inis *m.* whirlwind

turma -ae *f.* squadron, troop

turpo -āre stain, spoil

turriger -gera -gerum *adj.*

tower-bearing
turris -is *f.* tower
tūtus -a -um *adj.* safe
tuus -a -um *adj.* your, thy
tyrannus -i *m.* king, lord

ubi *conj.* where; when
ullus -a -um *adj.* any
ultor -ōris *m.* avenger
ultrā *adv.* farther
ultro *adv.* of one's own accord; even (830)
umbo -ōnis *m.* boss (of a shield)
umbra -ae *f.* shade, shadow
umerus -i *m.* shoulder
umquam *or* **unquam** *adv.* ever
ūnā *adv.* together; at the same time
unda -ae *f.* wave; water
unde *conj.* from where
undique *adv.* from all sides
undo -āre flow, stream
ūnus -a -um *adj.* one
urbs urbis *f.* city
urgeo -ēre ursi press forward; press hard
usquam *adv.* anywhere
usque *adv.* ever
ut *conj.* how (20): as (454): when (441, 570): *in wishes* would that (631)
uterque utraque utrumque each; both

vacat *impersonal* it is allowed; there is time for (625)
vadum -i *n.* shallow; wave; water
vāgīna -ae *f.* scabbard, sheath
valeo -ēre have the strength; be able
validus -a -um *adj.* strong, stout

vallus -i *m.* stake; *in pl.* stockade
vānus -a -um *adj.* vain; empty; devoid of (631)
varius -a -um *adj.* varied; divided
vastus -a -um *adj.* vast, enormous, huge
-ve *conj.* or
-ve...-ve either...or
veho -ere vexi vectum carry
vel *conj.* or
vel...vel either...or
vello -ere velli vulsum tear, pull up; pluck out (889)
vēlo -āre veil
vēlum -i *n.* sail
velut *adv.* just as, like
venēnum -i *n.* poison
venia -ae *f.* pardon; favour (626)
venio -īre vēni ventum come
ventus -i *m.* wind, gale
verber -eris *n.* lash, whip
verbero -āre beat, lash
verbum -i *n.* word
vēro *adv.* indeed
versicolor -ōris *adj.* of various colours
verso -āre debate; turn over (*in the mind*)
vertex -icis *m.* head, summit
verto -ere verti versum turn; change; overthrow (512); churn (208); *in pass.* depend (529)
vērum -i *n.* truth
vērus -a -um *adj.* true
vēsānus -a -um *adj.* mad; furious
vester -ra -rum *adj.* your
vestīgium -i *n.* footstep
vestis -is *f.* dress
vetitum -i *n.* prohibition
vetus -eris *adj.* old, ancient
vetustas -ātis *f.* antiquity

vetustus -a -um *adj.* ancient
via -ae *f.* way, road
viātor -ōris *c.* traveller
vibro -āre quiver
victor -ōris *m.* conqueror
victōria -ae *f.* victory
video -ēre vīdi vīsum see; see to it, decide (744)
videor -ēri vīsus seem
vigilo -āre be awake
vinco -ere vīci victum conquer
vinculum -i *n.* bond, chain
violentus -a -um *adj.* violent; furious
vir viri *m.* man; hero
virtus -ūtis *f.* courage
vīs *acc.* **vim** *f.* violence, force; influence (614)
vīres -ium *f.* strength
viscera -um *n.pl.* entrails
vīsus -ūs *m.* look, glance; sight
vīta -ae *f.* life
vitta -ae *f.* ribbon
vīvidus -a -um *adj.* lively, active
vīvo -ere vixi victum live, be alive
vix *adv.* scarcely

vōciferor -āri shout
voco -āre call, summon
volito -āre flit
volo velle volui wish; be willing
volo -āre fly
volucer -cris -cre *adj.* winged, flying
volucris -is *f.* bird
voluptas -ātis *f.* pleasure
voluto -āre roll about; ponder over (159)
volvo -ere -vi volūtum roll; *in pass.* roll about (700)
vomo -ere -ui -itum vomit forth
vorāgo -inis *f.* pit, gulf, whirlpool
vōs *pron.* you *pl.*
vōtum -i *n.* wish; prayer
voveo -ēre vōvi vōtum vow
vox vōcis *f.* voice; word
vulgo -āre publish; lay open
vulnus -eris *n.* wound
vultus -ūs *m.* face; expression

zephyrus -i *m.* west wind

Proper Names

Note: all those labelled 'Latin' are allies of Turnus.

Abas -antis *m.*	Etruscan ally of Aeneas
Achātes -ae *m.*	Aeneas' faithful friend
Achilles -is *and* -i *m.*	son of Peleus and Thetis. Most famous Greek hero at Troy
Achīvi -ōrum *or* -um *m.pl.*	Greeks
Acmōn -onis *m.*	an ally of Aeneas
Acron -ōnis *m.*	a Greek exile, ally of Aeneas
Aegaeon -ōnis *m.*	a giant
Aenēas -ae *m.*	son of Venus and Anchises. Mythical ancestor of the Romans
Aeneades -ae *m.*	follower of Aeneas. A Trojan
Aenēïus -a -um *adj.*	of Aeneas
Aeolia -ae *f.*	an island N.E. of Sicily. Home of the winds
Aetōlus -a -um *adj.*	of Aetolia. Aetolian
Āgis -idis *m.*	Lycian ally of Aeneas
Alcānor -oris *m.*	a Latin
Alcathous -i *m.*	a Trojan
Alcīdes -ae *m.*	descendant of Alceus. Hercules
Allecto -ūs *f.*	one of the three Furies
Alpes -ium *f.pl.*	the Alps
Alphēus -a -um *adj.*	of Alpheus, a river in Elis
Amathūs -untis *f.*	town in Cyprus, sacred to Venus

114

Amor -ōris *m.*	Love: Cupid
Amyclae -ārum *f.pl.*	a town in Latium
Amycus -i *m.*	a Trojan
Anchemolus -i *m.*	a Latin
Anchīses -ae *m.*	father of Aeneas
Anchīsiades -ae *m.*	son of Anchises. Aeneas
Antaeus -i *m.*	a Latin
Antōres -ae *m.*	companion of Heracles, ally of Aeneas
Anxur -uris *m.*	a Latin
Apollo -inis *m.*	the god Apollo. A ship's figurehead
Arcadia -ae *f.*	district in the Peloponnese
Arcadius -a -um *adj.*	Arcadian
Arcas -adis *adj. and noun*	Arcadian. An Arcadian
Argi -ōrum *m.pl.*	Argos, town in N.E. Peloponnese
Argolicus -a -um *adj.*	Argive. Greek
Arpi -ōrum *m.pl.*	a town in Apulia
Ascanius -i *m.*	son of Aeneas
Asia -ae *f.*	Asia
Asīlas -ae *m.*	an Etruscan seer, ally of Aeneas
Āsius -i *m.*	a Trojan
Assaracus -i *m.*	a Trojan
Astur -uris *m.*	an Etruscan ally of Aeneas
Aulestes -ae *m.*	an Etruscan, brother of Ocnus and ally of Aeneas
Aurōra -ae *f.*	goddess of Morning. Dawn
Aurunca -ae *f.*	Aurunca, a town in Campania
Ausonia -ae *f.*	Ancient name for Italy
Ausonidae -ārum *and* -um *m.pl.*	people of Ausonia. Italians
Ausonius -a -um *adj.*	of Ausonia. Italian
Ausonius -i *m.*	an Italian
Bēnācus -i *m.*	a lake from which the Mincius flows

Boreās -ae *m.*   the North Wind

Caeculus -i *m.*   son of Vulcan. Ally of Turnus
Caedicus -i *m.*   a Latin
Caere *abl.* Caerete *m.*   a town in Etruria
Camers -tis *m.*   a Latin
Campānus -a -um *adj.*   of Campania, an Italian province

Capys -yos *m.*   ally of Aeneas
Cassandra -ae *f.*   prophetess daughter of Priam and Hecuba

Castor -oris *m.*   a Trojan
Centaurus -i *m.*   a half-man, half-horse monster. A ship's figurehead

Chalybes -um *m.pl.*   a people who lived on the Black Sea coast and were noted for working in iron

Cinyrus -i *m.*   a leader of the Ligurians
Cissēis -idis *f.*   daughter of Cisseus. Hecuba, wife of Priam

Cisseus -ei *m.*   a Latin
Clarus -i *m.*   a Trojan
Clausus -i *m.*   ally of Turnus
Clonius -i *m.*   a Trojan
Clonus -i *m.*   a metal-work artist
Clūsium -i *n.*   a town in Etruria
Clūsīnus -a -um *adj.*   of Clusium
Clytius -i *m.*   (line 129) ally of Aeneas
Clytius -i *m.*   (line 325) a Latin
Corythus -i *m.*   a town in Etruria
Cosae -ārum *f.pl.*   a town in Etruria
Cronius -i *m.*   a Trojan
Cupāvo -ōnis *m.*   a Ligurian leader
Cures -ium *m.pl.*   chief town of the Sabines
Cybēle -es *or* -ae *f.*   Cybele, a Phrygian goddess
Cycnus -i *m.*   a Ligurian king, changed to a swan

Cȳdon -ōnis *m*.	a Latin
Cȳmodocēa -ae *f*.	a sea nymph
Cythēra -ōrum *n.pl*.	island off S. Greece, sacred to Venus
Dardanides *gen.pl*.	
Dardanidum *m*.	a descendant of Dardanus, a Trojan. Aeneas
Dardanius -a -um *adj*.	Trojan
Daucius -a -um *adj*.	of Daucus
Daunus -i *m*.	father of Turnus
Dēmodocus -i *m*.	Arcadian ally of Aeneas
Dindyma -ōrum *n.pl*.	a mountain in Mysia
Diomēdes -is *m*.	Greek hero at Troy
Dolichāon -onis *m*.	a Trojan
Dryope -es *f*.	a nymph
Dryops -pis *m*.	ally of Aeneas
Ericaetes -ae *m*.	a Trojan
Erycinus -a -um *adj*.	of Eryx, a mountain in Sicily
Etruscus -i *m*.	an Etruscan
Etruscus -a -um *adj*.	of Etruria. Etruscan
Euander -ri *m*.	Evander. An Arcadian who emigrated to Italy. Ally of Aeneas
Euandrius -a -um *adj*.	of Evander
Euanthes -ae *m*.	a Phrygian ally of Aeneas
Eurōpa -ae *f*.	Europe
Eurytides -ae *m*.	son of Eurytus
Faunus -i *m*.	God of shepherds and agriculture
Gradīvus -i *m*.	A name for the god Mars
Graius -a -um *adj*.	Greek
Graīī -ōrum *or* -um *m.pl*.	Greeks

Graviscae -ārum *f.pl.*	a town in Etruria
Gyas -ae *m.*	a Latin
Haemonides -ae *m.*	a Latin
Halaesus -i *m.*	ally of Turnus and chief of the Aurunci
Hebrus -i *m.*	a Trojan
Helicon -ōnis *m.*	mountain in Boeotia, sacred to the Muses
Hercules -is *m.*	son of Jupiter, deified after death
Hicetāonius -i *m.*	son of Hicetaon, a Trojan
Hisbo -ōnis *m.*	a Latin
Hydaspes -is *m.*	ally of Aeneas
Īda -ae *f.*	mountain near Troy. Ship's figurehead
Īdaeus -a -um *adj.*	of Ida
Īdalia -ae *f.*	same as Idalium
Īdalium -i *n.*	city in Cyprus, sacred to Venus
Īdas -ae *m.*	a Thracian
Īliacus -a -um *adj.*	of Ilium. Trojan
Īlus -i *m.*	a Latin
Ilva -ae *f.*	the island of Elba
Imāon -onis *m.*	ally of Turnus
Imbrasides -ae *m.*	son of Imbrasus, a Trojan
Īris -idis *f.*	messenger of the gods
Ismarus -a -um *adj.*	of Ismara, a city in Thrace
Ismarus -i *m.*	a Lydian, ally of Aeneas
Ītali -ōrum *or* -um *m.pl.*	Italians
Ītalia -ae *f.*	Italy
Ītalus -a -um *adj.*	Italian
Ītalus -i *m.*	an Italian
Iūlus -i *m.*	another name for Ascanius
Iūno -ōnis *f.*	Juno, wife and sister of Jupiter
Iuppiter Iovis *m.*	Jupiter, ruler of gods and men

Karthāgo -inis *f.*	Carthage, a city in N. Africa
Lādon -ōnis *m.*	an Arcadian ally of Aeneas
Lagus -i *m.*	a Latin
Lārīdes -ae *m.*	a Latin
Latagus -i *m.*	ally of Aeneas
Latīni -ōrum *m.pl.*	the Latins
Latīnus -i *m.*	King of Latium
Latīnus -a -um *adj.*	Latin, of Latium
Latium -i *n.*	a country in Italy
Laurens -entis *adj.*	of Laurentum, a Latin town
Laurentius -a -um *adj.*	of Laurentum
Lausus -i *m.*	son of Mezentius, ally of Turnus
Lichas -ae *m.*	a Latin
Liger -is *m.*	a Latin
Ligures -um *m.pl.*	an Italian people, allies of Aeneas
Lūcagus -i *m.*	a Latin
Lūcas -ae *m.*	a Latin
Lycāonius -a -um *adj.*	of Lycaon, an Arcadian king
Lycia -ae *f.*	a country in Asia Minor
Lycius -a -um *adj.*	Lycian
Lȳdius -a -um *adj.*	Lydian
Lyrnēsius -a -um *adj.*	of Lyrnesus, a town in the Troad
Maeon -onis *m.*	a Latin
Maeonius -a -um *adj.*	of Maeonia in Lydia
Magus -i *m.*	a Latin
Manto -ūs *f.*	mother of Ocnus, founder of Mantua
Mantua -ae *f.*	city on River Mincius. Virgil's birth-place
Mars Martis *m.*	god of War. Warfare
Marsi -ōrum *m.pl.*	a Latin people

Massicus -i *m*.	Etruscan ally of Aeneas
Māvors *m*.	same as Mars
Melampus -i *m*.	a companion of Hercules
Menestheūs -ei *m*.	a Trojan
Messāpus -i *m*.	son of Neptune. Ally of Turnus
Mezentius -i *m*.	an exiled Etruscan tyrant, allied to Turnus
Mimas -antis *m*.	a Trojan, friend of Paris
Mincius -i *m*.	tributary of the River Po. A ship's figurehead
Minio -onis *m*.	a river in Etruria
Mnestheūs -ei *m*.	ally of Aeneas
Mūsa -ae *f*.	One of the nine goddesses of the arts
Nealces -is *m*.	a Trojan
Neptūnius -a -um *adj*.	of Neptune, god of the sea
Nēreūs -ei *and* -eos *m*.	a sea-god. The sea
Niphaeus -i *m*.	a Latin
Numa -ae *m*.	a Latin
Numitor -ōris *m*.	a Latin
Ocnus -i *m*.	an Etruscan, founder of Mantua
Olympus -i *m*.	a mountain in Thessaly, the abode of the gods.
Ōricius -a -um *adj*.	of Oricum in Illyria
Orion -onis *m*.	a famous hunter. After death placed as a constellation in the sky
Orōdes -is *m*.	a Trojan
Orses -ae *m*.	a Trojan
Osinius -i *m*.	King of Clusium, ally of Aeneas
Pactōlus -i *m*.	river in Lydia said to carry down golden sand

Pallas -antis *m.*	son of Evander. Ally of Aeneas
Palmus -i *m.*	ally of Aeneas
Paphus *and* -os *f.*	town in Cyprus with a temple of Venus
Parca -ae *f.*	one of the three Fates
Paris -idis *m.*	son of Priam and Hecuba. Carried off Helen from Sparta
Parthenius -i *m.*	a Trojan
Pergama -ōrum *n.pl.*	the citadel of Troy. Troy
Phaethon -ōntis *m.*	son of the Sun god. Killed by Jupiter's thunderbolt
Pharus -i *m.*	a Latin
Pheres -etis *m.*	Arcadian ally of Aeneas
Phoebē -es *f.*	the Moon goddess. Diana
Phoebus -i *m.*	a name for the god Apollo
Phorcus -i *m.*	a Latin
Phryges -um *m.pl.*	Phrygians
Phrygia -ae *f.*	a country in Asia Minor
Phrygius -a -um *adj.*	Phrygian
Pīlumnus -i *m.*	a Latin deity. Ancestor of Turnus
Pīsae -ārum *f.pl.*	a town in Etruria
Populōnia -ae *f.*	a town in Etruria
Pyrgi -ōrum *m.pl.*	a town in Etruria
Rapo -ōnis *m.*	a Latin
Rhaebus -i *m.*	the horse of Mezentius
Rhoetēus -ei *and* -eos *m.*	a Latin
Rhoetus -i *m.*	King of the Marsians
Rōma -ae *f.*	Rome
Rōmānus -a -um *adj.*	Roman
Rutuli -ōrum *m.pl.*	Rutulians, a Latin tribe whose king was Turnus
Rutulus -a -um *adj.*	Rutulian
Rutulus -i *m.*	a Rutulian

Sacrātor -ōris *m*.	a Latin
Salius -i *m*.	a Latin
Sarpēdon -onis *m*.	son of Jupiter, killed in Trojan War
Saturnius -a -um *adj*.	of Saturn: descended from Saturn
Serestus -i *m*.	a Trojan
Simois -entis *m*.	a river near Troy
Sīrius -a -um *adj*.	of Sirius, the Dogstar
Sparta -ae *f*.	capital of Laconia. Home of Menelaus and Helen
Sthenelus -i *m*.	a Latin
Strȳmonius -a -um *adj*.	of the River Strymon
Strȳmonius -i *m*.	an Arcadian
Stygius -a -um *adj*.	of the Styx, river in the Underworld
Sulmo -ōnis *m*.	a follower of Turnus
Syrtis -is *f*.	sandbank off N. African coast
Tarchon -ontis *m*.	an Etruscan ally of Aeneas
Tarquitus -i *m*.	a Latin
Teucri -ōrum *and* -um *m.pl*.	Trojans
Teuthras -antis *m*.	ally of Aeneas
Thaemon -ōnis *m*.	Lycian ally of Aeneas
Theano -ūs *f*.	wife of Amycus
Thēron -ōnis *m*.	a Latin
Thoas -antis *m*.	Arcadian ally of Aeneas
Thrēïcius -a -um *adj*.	Thracian
Thronius -i *m*.	a Trojan
Thȳbris -is *or* -idis *m*.	river Tiber
Thymber -ri *m*.	a Latin
Thymbris -is *m*.	a Trojan
Thymoētes -ae *m*.	a Trojan
Tiberīnus -a -um *adj*.	of the River Tiber
Tigris -is *or* -idis *f*.	tigress. A ship's figurehead
Tīsiphone -es *f*.	one of the three Furies

Trīton -onis *m*.	a sea-god. A ship's figurehead
Trivia -ae *f*.	goddess of three ways. Diana
Trōes -um *m.pl*.	Trojans
Troia -ae *f*.	Troy
Troiānus -a -um *adj*.	Trojan
Troiānus -i *m*.	a Trojan
Trōius -a -um *adj*.	a Trojan
Trōs Trōis *m*.	a Trojan
Turnus -i *m*.	King of the Rutuli. Arch enemy of Aeneas
Tuscus -a -um *adj*.	Etruscan
Tȳdīdes -ae *m*.	son of Tydeus. Diomedes
Tyres -ae *m*.	ally of Aeneas
Tyrius -a -um *adj*.	Tyrian. Carthaginian
Tyrrhēnus -a -um *adj*.	Etruscan
Ūfens -entis *m*.	a Latin
Umbro -ōnis *m*.	chief of the Marsi, ally of Turnus
Valerus -i *m*.	a Latin
Venīlia -ae *f*.	mother of Turnus
Venus -eris *f*.	goddess of Love. Mother of Aeneas.
Vesulus -i *m*.	a mountain in Liguria
Volcānius -a -um *adj*.	of Vulcan
Volcānus -i *m*.	Roman god of fire
Volcens -entis *m*.	father of Camers, a Rutulian
Xanthus -i *m*.	a river near Troy